MANNERS of the HEART

Heart Education Curriculum

GRADE 3

Baton Rouge, LA

Published by **MANNERS** of the **HEART**

763 North Boulevard
Baton Rouge, LA 70802
225.383.3235
www.mannersoftheheart.org

Second Edition
Copyright 2019 by **MANNERS** of the **HEART**
All rights reserved.
Printed in the United States of America.

Author: Jill Rigby Garner
Editor: Angelle High
Editor at large: Angelle Roddy
Graphic Design: Shelby Bailey
Cover Design: Brian Rivet
Merryville Stories: Nick and Jill Garner, Micah Webber
Contributor: Emily Jones
Photography: Darlene Aguillard, McCauley Mills, Taylor Frey

MANNERS of the **HEART** grants teachers the right to photocopy the reproducibles from this book for classroom use. No other part of this publication may be reproduced, stored in a retrieval system, or transmitted in any form or by any means—electronic, mechanical, photocopy, recording, or any other, without the prior written permission of the publisher. Please direct all questions and inquiries to:

info@mannersoftheheart.org or
MANNERS of the **HEART**
763 North Boulevard
Baton Rouge, LA 70802
www.mannersoftheheart.org

TABLE OF CONTENTS

ACKNOWLEDGEMENTS — 5

INTRODUCTION — 6

UNIT 1: ATTITUDES OF THE HEART

WEEK 1   Welcome to Merryville — 12
Manners

WEEK 2   Introducing Good Deeds — 18
Respect

WEEK 3   Choosing Respect — 24
Goodness & Respect

WEEK 4   Helping Others — 30
Kindness & Love

WEEK 5   Forgiving Others — 36
Patience & Humility

WEEK 6   Appreciating Others — 42
Encouragement & Appreciation

WEEK 7   Being a Buddy, Not a Bully — 48
Acceptance & Kindness

WEEK 8   Following the Golden Rule — 54
Empathy & Humility

UNIT 2: EVERYDAY COURTESIES

WEEK 9   Becoming Ladies and Gentlemen — 60
Gentle & Gracious

WEEK 10   Being a Host — 66
Hospitality & Generosity

WEEK 11   Being a Guest — 72
Grateful & Polite

TABLE OF CONTENTS

UNIT 3: COMMUNICATION SKILLS

WEEK 12	Greetings and Introductions *Friendliness & Maturity*	78
WEEK 13	Encouraging Conversation *Self-control & Participation*	84
WEEK 14	Using the Phone *Responsibility & Courtesy*	90
WEEK 15	Writing from the Heart *Thoughtful & Expressive*	96

UNIT 4: LIVING IN COMMUNITY

WEEK 16	Respecting Adults *Honor & Obedience*	102
WEEK 17	Respecting the Team *Cooperation & Sportsmanship*	108
WEEK 18	Respecting Differences *Understanding & Acceptance*	114
WEEK 19	Respecting Privacy *Considerate & Trustworthy*	120
WEEK 20	Respecting Property *Appreciation & Responsibility*	126
WEEK 21	Respecting Your Community *Civil & Appropriate*	132
WEEK 22	Respecting Our Country *Patriotism & Citizenship*	138
WEEK 23	Respecting Our Environment *Conscientious & Resourceful*	144

GLOSSARY	151
REPRODUCIBLES	155
Student Activity Sheets	156
Home Connection Letters	213

ACKNOWLEDGEMENTS

CONTRIBUTORS

Thank you to those who contributed to the revision and expansion of this curriculum— teachers, schools, staff and friends.

Angelle High	Angelle Roddy	Emily Jones
Ashton Camper	Sandra Slater	Wes Mainord
Katherine Chenevert	Diane Jones	Nick Garner
Anita Hebert	Angela Jones	Loren Barilleau

Manners of the Heart Students everywhere

John Smith, S & S Printing, LLC

Photography: Darlene Aguillard, McCauley Mills, Taylor Frey

SUPPORTERS

Manners of the Heart Board of Directors

The Emerson & Barbara Kampen Foundation

The Powell Group Fund

Manners of the Heart Support Team

TECHNOLOGY & ANIMATION

Interactive Board Activities: Anna Price

"Wilbur Goes to School" & "Good Deeds": LUMA, Inc., Morgan Krutz
    Crew: Leo Harelson, Chase Champagne, Jason Nystrom, Baylor Hood,
        Collin Sweat, Cricket Nystrom
    Cast: Ray Gaspard, Benjamin Lee, Clay Young, Andrew Moock, David Gary
    Music: Harold Mims

Special Thanks to:
Principal Mike Stiglets, Parkview Elementary School, Oklahoma City, OK
Highland Elementary School, Baton Rouge, LA

INTRODUCTION

Big Ideas

- Unlocking the heart opens the mind.
- Children who learn to esteem others, gain respect for themselves.
- Self-esteem must be replaced with self-respect.

For Your Heart

Would you agree your students need the following attributes in their hearts?

Too often in today's world, our students' hearts look more like this:

In the early 1970s, specialists began telling us the secret to educating children was to build their self-esteem. Books on the subject skyrocketed to the top of best-seller lists, encouraging us to be friends with children rather than their authority figures. Discipline was out, and praise was in. We stopped encouraging children to persevere until they achieved greatness. Instead, we told them they were the best. The "sticker revolution" began.

Today we are faced with plummeting test scores, escalating violence, among even our youngest students, paralyzing entitlement and epidemic levels of disrespect. The evidence is clear—self-esteem was not the cure, but rather the culprit.

For the Hearts of Your Students

Manners of the Heart was developed to help you teach your students to respect and esteem others, and in the process, gain respect for themselves. Self-esteem is replaced with self-respect, enabling them to see beyond themselves and their circumstances.

Through this process, your students will learn how to self-regulate their behavior. The intrinsic quality of self-respect translates into motivated, self-disciplined children with a desire to learn and a longing to become all they are meant to be.

As an educator, you have the distinct privilege of unlocking the hearts of your students so their minds will open to receive the knowledge you have to impart to them.

INSTRUCTIONAL DESIGN

Lev Vygotsky, a developmental psychologist in the early 1900s, introduced the foundation for what has become the social and emotional learning of today. The necessity of social interactions, instruction and relationships in the development of higher learning was a cornerstone of his work. He asserted that the potential for cognitive development is limited without fully developed social skills.

In the scope and sequence of Manners of the Heart lessons, we have designed three levels of competency based on Vygotsky's Social Development Theory. Weekly lessons expand by grade level to include the ever-changing world of a child.

Helping when asked — LEVEL 1 COMPETENCY PreK - 1st

Helping without being asked — LEVEL 2 COMPETENCY 2nd - 3rd

Helping by teaching — LEVEL 3 COMPETENCY 4th - 5th

Using Week 4 as an example, the concept of Helping Others is introduced as "Helping when asked to help." The world of PreK-1st graders consists of a small, protected environment. Learning how to follow directions is the first level of competency.

As their world expands, 2nd & 3rd graders begin to understand the next level of competency, "Helping without being asked."

The satisfaction gained from following the direction to help others in their early years, becomes the motivation to reach out and help someone who is in need without being asked.

In 4th & 5th grade, the third and highest level of competency of Helping Others is achieved when "Helping by teaching" is understood as the best way of truly helping someone. When this level of competency in social and emotional skills is reached, a child's attitudes and actions are carried into adulthood.

Your students will discover that the greatest satisfaction in life comes from finding your purpose so that you can help others find their purpose. This is the long-term gain and life-transforming work in the heart of your students that takes place through Manners of the Heart.

2013-2014 University Research Study

Dr. Monique LeBlanc, Ph.D., Professor of Psychology at Southeastern Louisiana University, conducted a research study on the academic impact of Manners of the Heart® in schools.

-30% Decrease in Disciplinary Referrals

+15pt Increase in SPS

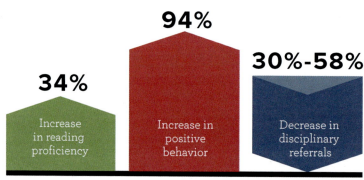

- 34% Increase in reading proficiency
- 94% Increase in positive behavior
- 30%-58% Decrease in disciplinary referrals

What Manners of the Heart Schools Say

MATERIALS & RESOURCES

You'll Need:

- Grade Level Teacher's Manual or Blackline Masters Binder (Contains reproducible worksheets and Home Connection Letters)
- Grade Level Student Workbooks
- Wilbur, Peter and Penelope Puppets
- Happle Tree Poster and Happles
- Character Set for Bulletin Boards
- Heart Attribute Flashcards

DIGITAL RESOURCES

MY MANNERS

My Manners is the digital portal available with paid subscription at mannersoftheheart.org

- Grade Level Lesson Materials and Reproducibles
- 161 Interactive Whiteboard Activities—designed for use with ActivInspire Software
- Look for this icon! It indicates availability of an online resource for lesson enhancement.
- Audio Theatre Recordings of the Merryville Stories
- Video Recordings of Merryville
- Songs
- Animation Videos
- Daily Morning Announcements
- Journal Prompts
- English and Spanish Home Connection Letters
- Graphics
- Assessment Forms and Award Certificates
- Grade-Level Reading Lists

BEST PRACTICE

Manners of the Heart is an effective, user-friendly SEL curriculum for your students. For optimum results, incorporate Days 1-5 of the Manners of the Heart Curriculum. Introduce the Concept on Day 1 and obtain Mastery by Day 5.

DELIVERY OF INSTRUCTION

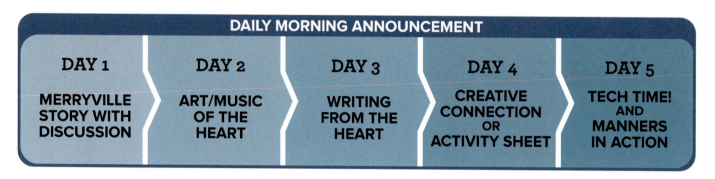

Daily Morning Announcement—Begin each day with these words of encouragement.

Day 1 **Merryville Story with Discussion**—Read aloud or play audio recording.
Heart Attributes—Character qualities emphasized in the lesson.
Manners in Action—Charge to students to incorporate Heart Attributes in daily life.

Day 2 **Art/Music of the Heart**—Reinforces concepts with visual art or musical activity.

Day 3 **Writing from the Heart**—Journal prompt for creative writing assignment.

Day 4 **Creative Connection**—Reinforces concepts with puppet play, drama or creative play.

Day 5 **Tech Time!**—Have fun and learn with an Interactive Board Activity.
Manners in Action—Encourages students to share their experiences and then hang the Heart Attributes (Happles) on the Happle Tree.

REINFORCEMENT AT HOME

Weekly Home Connection Letters—Each lesson comes with a Home Connection Letter that gives parents and guardians a glimpse into what is being taught in the classroom. Families will find practical tips and suggestions for integration and reinforcement in the home.

ENGAGING THE IMAGINATION

At Manners of the Heart, we believe the imagination is born from the heart. The first step toward academic success is unlocking the hearts of your students so their minds will open to receive the information you have to impart to them. Weekly lessons are story-based and set in the fictitious town of Merryville, which is filled with comical characters and creative story lines that illustrate the principles being taught in each lesson.

MERRYVILLE'S MAIN CHARACTERS

Wise Ol' Wilbur   Buddy   Bully   Sketch

Henry   Peter   Penelope   BillyBeeRight

HEART ATTRIBUTES

Wilbur, the Wise Ol' Owl, lives in the **Happle Tree**, the only one like it in the world! **Happles** grow on Wilbur's tree, each representing an individual *Heart Attribute*. With every lesson, Happles are added to the Happle Tree. As the tree fills with Happles, so a child's heart fills with all good things!

Wilbur's Glossary (found in the back of the manual) provides original definitions, which encourage vocabulary, as well as character growth!

WEEK 1
WELCOME TO MERRYVILLE

Big Ideas

- Manners are the foundation for morals.
- Manners are not a set of rules to be followed, but rather principles that guide behavior.
- The attitude behind the action determines the action.

For Your Heart

It has been said that educating the mind without educating the heart is no education at all. Manners of the Heart couldn't agree more. During our "Listen to the Children" study, we interviewed more than 400 children, ages five to fourteen from different backgrounds. Using questions ranging from "Do you like chores?" to "What is a family?" the children's answers were enlightening. One such question, "What's more important, being smart or being nice?" elicited enlightening *and convicting* answers. 96% of the children responded without hesitation, "Nice." Other responses:

- "I want to be nice because that will make me smart."
- "If you're not nice, then you're not smart."
- "I must be smart 'cause I try to be nice."

These children know that head knowledge and heart knowledge cannot be separated from each other, but this is what we too often attempt to do! Just imagine how wonderful your classroom will be this year when you equip your students with not only head knowledge to lead, but also heart knowledge to lead in the right direction! You'll have a room full of eager learners ready to lead!

For the Hearts of Your Students

Our mission is to provide you with a professional heart education curriculum designed to strengthen morals, improve social and emotional skills, and increase respectfulness, thereby helping you develop character in your students.

The core values taught through Manners of the Heart are the following:

- Manners are defined as an attitude of the heart that is self-giving, not self-serving.
- Manners are rooted in respect for others.

In this week's lesson, you'll be introducing your students to the true meaning of *manners* through "Welcome to Merryville". Through the story, you'll begin the process of instilling *manners* in the hearts of your students, while engaging their imaginations. As they visit Merryville, they'll meet characters who teach them how to put the heart attributes they will acquire this year into action in their daily lives.

1 Welcome to Merryville

MANNERS—An attitude of the heart that puts the needs of others ahead of my own

REMEMBER

SKILLS AND OBJECTIVES

- Students will be introduced to or reacquainted with the town of Merryville.
- Students will be introduced to or reacquainted with Wise Ol' Wilbur and his Happle Tree.
- Students will consider the true meaning and motivation behind manners.

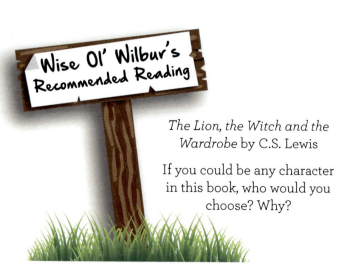

The Lion, the Witch and the Wardrobe by C.S. Lewis

If you could be any character in this book, who would you choose? Why?

GUIDING CHILDREN'S LEARNING

1. Introduce the *Heart Attribute* of MANNERS and its definition. Every week will begin with *Heart Attributes* followed by a *Merryville story*. Encourage students to listen for the *Heart Attributes* in each story.
2. Before the story, show the students the **Map of Merryville**.
3. Read aloud or listen to the recording of **Albert and the Happle Tree**
4. After listening to the story, lead your students in a discussion:
   - *Who is Albert McDonald?*
     He is Mrs. McDonald's husband's great-great-grandfather.
   - *When Albert refused to share his candy with his friend, how do you think his friend felt?*
     Sad, upset, disappointed, lonely.
   - *Who lives in the Happle Tree?*
     Wilbur, the Wise Ol' Owl lives in the Happle Tree.
   - *When Albert found and ate the happle, what changed?*
     Albert's heart changed. He realized he had been selfish and needed to treat others the way he would want to be treated.
   - *Have you ever felt like Albert and not wanted to share with another person?* (Answers will vary.)
   - *What is the Golden Rule? How does Albert's lesson of the Golden Rule relate to us?*
     The Golden Rule means to treat others the way you want to be treated. Albert's lesson can remind us to put others before ourselves and be respectful because it is what we would want.

MANNERS IN ACTION

1. *Manners in Action* is an opportunity to carefully consider the *Heart Attributes* of the week and to put them into action. Look again at the definition of MANNERS and encourage students to memorize it.
2. Introduce the **Happle Tree** poster and **Happles**. At the end of this week, the MANNERS Happle will be hung, displaying the *Heart Attribute* of the week. As the Happle Tree grows with Happles throughout the year, it becomes a picture of the growth in the hearts of the students.
3. Discuss these *Big Ideas*:
   - *MANNERS come from the heart.*
   - *When we consider the needs of others before our own needs, we will treat them well.*
   - *The way we treat others is a reflection of the attitudes of our hearts.*
4. Challenge your students to truly consider how they are treating others this week. If they find themselves being unkind or even wanting to bully someone, ask them to look inside and consider the attitudes within their hearts. *At the end of the week, those who have been carefully watching how they treat others will be recognized and will possibly hang the first Happle on the Happle Tree!*

Day 1

ALBERT AND THE HAPPLE TREE

Once upon a heart in Merryville, Tommy and his friends had been fishing all day. Before they headed home, they decided to stop by Mrs. McDonald's house to say hello. Wouldn't you know it; she was just taking her famous cookies out of the oven. Before they could ask, she invited them in for a snack.

Tommy took one bite of those cookies and said, "Mrs. McDonald, these really are the best chocolate chip cookies I ever tasted."

"Glad you like 'em, Tommy. It's an old family recipe," replied Mrs. McDonald. "How old?" quizzed Tommy. "Well, so old, I don't know how old," chuckled Mrs. McDonald.

"Sounds like the Happle Tree. Nobody knows how old it is either," said Tommy. "That's right, Tommy, but did you know my great, great grandfather, Albert McDonald, discovered the Happle Tree when he was just a boy?" answered Mrs. McDonald.

"I didn't know that. Will you tell us the story?" Tommy asked. Mrs. McDonald began...

It was a cold wintry morning in Merryville. Snow had been falling for days. Christmas was only a week away. Little Albert's pop was busy in his workshop trying to finish a special Christmas gift—a new super-fast sled. He had spent long hours working on it. Albert often wondered who would receive the sled.

"Albert, time is running out. The runners still need to be painted. Would you do that today?" Albert's pop asked. Albert thought, "Why should I paint runners for someone else's sled?"

"Pop, I don't have time today. I'm going to town," answered Albert. "But, Albert, I really need your help," said Albert's pop. "Don't have time now, pop," Albert said, as he ran out of the workshop. Chester, Albert's faithful hound dog, came running from the barn to join him on the walk to town.

Albert and Chester passed an old man who was asking for money to help his family at Christmas. Albert slowed down, but instead of dropping money into the man's cup, he ran into Miss Charlotte's Chocolate Shoppe to buy some of his favorite ten-cent candy.

One of Albert's buddies came up to him in the chocolate shop and asked for a piece of his candy. "Not today," Albert replied. "But, Albert," said his friend, "I gave you some of my candy last week."

"Yeah, but you had a lot more candy than I do," Albert replied, and headed toward the door with two bars in his hand.

Running out of the chocolate shop, Albert bumped into a table and knocked a chocolate Santa Claus to the floor. Miss Charlotte didn't see it! Albert kept going without picking up the broken Santa Claus. "Let's go, Chester," Albert said. The two headed for their favorite walk through the woods.

Albert picked up a stick and threw it for Chester to fetch. Chester brought the stick back and Tommy threw it again, but this time he decided to run after Chester. Not looking where he was going, he tripped over something under the snow and fell to the ground. Chester jumped to help him. "Chester, I'm alright, boy. See if you can find out what's under there," said Albert as he pulled himself up from the snow.

Chester started sniffing and pawing in the snow. It didn't take long to find out what had tripped his master. Chester barked, as he pointed to the root of a giant tree hidden under days of snow.

Albert helped Chester clear the snow and trace the root of the great tree back to its trunk. "This thing is huge, Chester. It must be big around as a merry-go-round." What do you think?" asked Albert. Chester circled the tree and barked in agreement.

Towering over them stood a tree like no other. The leaves were a hundred shades of green and so thick they could hardly see the sky. The branches reached to the clouds and stretched across the river to rest on the other side. Hanging from the branches were bright red, heart-shaped balls.

Suddenly, they heard a call from the highest part of the tree, "Whooooo goes there?" From the top of the tree, an enormous owl swooped down to sit on the big branch in front of them. He was speckled grey with giant eyebrows that curved to his ears. His bright yellow beak looked like it had been painted. The owl spoke again, "I said, whooooo goes there?"

Surprised, but not scared, Albert answered, "I'm Albert McDonald and this here dog is Chester."

"Nice to meet you, Albert and Chester. I'm Wise Ol' Wilbur."

"Sir, can you tell me about this fine tree you're sittin' in? I've never seen a tree, the likes of this one," replied Albert. "That's because this is the only Happle Tree in the world," Wilbur said.

"Happle Tree? What's a happle?" Albert asked. "Happles are the fruit of my tree," Wilbur continued. "This is your tree?" Albert jumped in. "I've lived in this tree for a looooong, looooong time," answered Wilbur. "How long is that?" asked Albert.

"Forever and ever," said Wilbur as he plucked a happle from a branch. "Now, to answer your first question...A happle is a fruit filled with goodness that's shaped like a heart and tastes sweet as an apple. That's why they're called happles."

1 Welcome to Merryville

"They sure do look good to eat," said Albert. "They are good to eat, Albert, but they're not just good for your belly, they're good for your heart too," said Wilbur, putting on his glasses to look into Albert's heart. "Whooooo, I see trouble in there. Trouble, indeed," noted Wilbur.

"Wilbur, what do you mean, trouble in there?" asked Albert. "Well, Albert," answered Wilbur. "When I put on my glasses, I can see into boys' and girls' hearts."

"What do you see in my heart, Wilbur?" asked Albert. "I see a heart that needs to learn the Golden Rule. A heart that needs to learn how to treat others the way you want to be treated," answered Wilbur. "What do you mean?" asked Albert. "I see a broken chocolate Santa in Miss Charlotte's shop because you didn't stop to pick it up or apologize," said Wilbur. "But I was in a hurry," answered Albert. "I see you didn't share your candy with a friend who shared his candy with you last week," said Wilbur. "But he had more than I did," answered Albert. "I see an old man who needed help, but you didn't help him," said Wilbur. "But I needed my money to buy my favorite candy bars," answered Albert. "I see your father asking you for help building a sled, but you didn't have time," said Wilbur. Albert felt bad, but didn't know what to do.

"Albert, I suggest you try a happle for your heart," said Wilbur as he plucked a happle, polished it on his chest, and handed it to Albert. "A happle a day keeps the trouble away," added Wilbur.

Albert took a bite of the happle and said, "Mmmmmm, that is good. Let's go, Chester, we have a lot of work to do." On the way back to town, Albert decided he would apologize to Miss Charlotte and offer to help her make another chocolate Santa. And he decided to give his friend a bar of chocolate. But then thought, "No, I'll give him two." And he decided the homeless man needed the rest of his money.

When he returned home, his pop was not quite finished with the sled. Albert helped tighten the screws and polish the runners. When he finished, he headed off to bed.

Albert drifted off to sleep thinking of the things he had learned that day. *I learned to apologize, to share and to help others when they need it. Now I know how to treat others the way I want to be treated.*

As she finished the story, Mrs. McDonald said, "You see, Tommy, Albert never forgot the Christmas he learned the Golden Rule. On Christmas morning, Miss Charlotte surprised him with a chocolate Santa. His friend came by with a chocolate bar. And the sled he helped his pop finish, was a gift for Albert. In fact, the sled you use when you speed down Merryville Mountain is Albert's sled!"

Mrs. McDonald smiled and looked at the old sled leaning against the wall by the door, just waiting for the next run down the hill.

Just the beginning...

Day 2   ART OF THE HEART®

1. Give each student an activity sheet and ask them to describe one of the characters mentioned in **Albert and the Happle Tree**.

2. Illustrate the character in the picture box.

3. Write a paragraph describing the character.

4. Encourage your students to describe both the physical characteristics and the heart attitudes that they have imagined from hearing the story.

You'll Need:
- **My Merryville** activity sheet (1/student)
- Crayons
- Pencils

Days 2-5

Day 3 WRITING FROM THE HEART

Ask your students to consider the following journal prompt and answer it according to your classroom writing requirements:

When you are looking for a friend, what Heart Attribute do you think is most important? Why?

You'll Need:
- Welcome to Merryville activity sheet (1/student)

Day 4 CREATIVE CONNECTION

1. Remind students that *Heart Attributes* are the attitudes we want to develop in our hearts throughout the year.
2. Ask them to write the *Heart Attributes* they want to grow in this year.
3. Have students share what they have written and why.
4. Keep these activity sheets for the end of the year so your students can see how they have grown.

You'll Need:
- Manners in the Heart activity sheet (1/student)
- Pencils

Day 5 TECH TIME

Interactive Whiteboard Activity on MyManners Portal

Find out more about your favorite Merryville citizens!

MANNERS IN ACTION

Whooooo will hang the **Happle** this week?

MANNERS—An attitude of the heart that puts the needs of others ahead of my own

17

WEEK 2
INTRODUCING GOOD DEEDS

Big Ideas

- Following rules becomes an opportunity to perform good deeds when the motive behind the action is to help others.

- Learning to follow rules is an important part of learning and growing.

- Helping others learn and grow is a way for everyone to learn and grow.

For Your Heart

The primary goal of classroom management is to create an environment that fosters high achievement, both socially and academically. Identifying your students' individual personalities and learning styles is the beginning of developing a cooperative classroom that positions children to learn.

Establishing classroom rules is the next step in giving your students a sense of belonging and security. When you shift the focus from following rules to helping others, your basic rules become good deeds. At the heart of all good deeds is respect for others—the desire to protect the dignity of someone else by your attitude and actions.

You will be helping your students see how their actions affect their classmates' abilities to learn and grow.

For the Hearts of Your Students

Three simple classroom rules for your students to work toward are as follows:

- Keep your hands and feet to yourself.
- Raise your hand before talking in class.
- Follow your teacher's directions.

These rules give children the opportunity to do good deeds and experience the joy that comes through helping others learn and grow.

In this week's lesson, you will set in place the foundational principle of others-centeredness in your students' hearts. You will be instilling *respect* for others in your students, which will become the steadfast rule they live by as they venture into the world beyond your classroom.

2 Introducing Good Deeds

RESPECT—Treating others with dignity

REMEMBER

SKILLS AND OBJECTIVES

- Children will work together to create a *Classroom Constitution*.
- Children will learn why rules are important for learning and growing.
- Children will consider the *Declaration of Independence* and the *United States Constitution* as examples of documents for which sacrifices were made.

Clementine
by Sarah Pennypacker

What rules does Clementine have a difficult time following? Why are those rules helpful to her?

GUIDING CHILDREN'S LEARNING

1. Begin the lesson by introducing the *Heart Attribute* for the week, RESPECT. Encourage students to memorize and repeat the definition throughout the week.
2. It's Story Time! Read aloud or listen to the recording of **Declaration of Sacrifice**
3. After the story, lead your students in the following discussion:
    - *Who led the Merryville citizens in the procession to the beach?*
    Sergeant Joe
    - *What do we know about him?*
    Sergeant Joe is in a wheelchair. He bravely fought in a war and lost friends there.
    - *What document was signed in 1776?*
    The Declaration of Independence
    - *What document contains the laws for the United States of America?*
    The Constitution
    - *Caroline asked why men and women are willing to fight and die for people they don't know. What did Sergeant Joe say?*
    He said they fought so all could have freedom.
    - *How was Sergeant Joe showing RESPECT for his friends from the war?*
    He wanted people to remember their sacrifice when they lit the candles and sent them off.

MANNERS IN ACTION

1. Review the definition of the *Heart Attribute*, RESPECT.
2. Discuss these *Big Ideas* with your students:
    - Our nation was built many years ago when the Declaration of Independence and the Constitution were signed.
    - We will write our own Classroom Constitution together based on the principle of RESPECT.
    - We will sign and follow our Classroom Constitution based on the principle of RESPECT.
3. How can we demonstrate RESPECT? As your students walk through the process of brainstorming, writing and signing their own *Classroom Constitution*, encourage them to submit ideas that are based on RESPECT. Look for those students who are contributing for the good of everyone!

Day 1

DECLARATION OF SACRIFICE

Once upon a heart in Merryville, during the darkest hour of the evening, no one was sleeping. Main Street was empty, silent, smothered by a thick, velvety blanket of night. Save for a few lit windows, the only thing that was left shining in the little town was the reflection of the star-spangled sky. Not even the lighthouse beam interrupted the dark.

A long line of Merryville citizens wound slowly down the path around Ol' McDonald's farm to the lighthouse and the sea. Every now and then, there were snatches of conversation, but the townspeople were mostly hushed. Each family carried a small parcel. Caroline tugged on her father's sleeve and whispered, "Dad, why do we do this every year?"

Her dad's big, strong hand came down to rest on her back as they walked together, "A long, long time ago, before you were born, Sergeant Joe got the whole town together to institute a new tradition. I've been following this ritual since I was a little boy."

"But why?" she insisted.

"You know that Sergeant Joe fought in the war when he was far younger than I am now," her dad spoke quietly. "He lost many of his dearest friends over there. We go to remind ourselves of their sacrifice."

Caroline didn't know what to say to that. It seemed very serious and even a little difficult to understand. Why would someone who would never know her, sacrifice his life for her?

The townspeople drew within earshot of the ocean. Faintly at first, and then with growing strength, the roar of the ocean against the rocks could be detected. Caroline was still curious, so she left her dad and zig-zagged through the forest of people to the front of the column.

There she found Sergeant Joe, squeaking along ahead of everyone in his wheelchair. In his lap was the same type of parcel everyone else was carrying. He looked up at her as she came beside him and smiled a greeting.

"Hey," she said sheepishly.

"Good evening," he said warmly.

Caroline felt awkward asking, but she didn't know how else to get her question across. She faltered and then dove in, "Sergeant Joe, why did you fight?"

He smiled again, this time looking into the distance. He took a really long time to answer, so long that Caroline wondered if he had forgotten the question.

"Can I tell you a story?" he asked. Caroline nodded.

"In the summer of 1776, before we were even a nation, a few brave men decided to declare independence from Great Britain because they wanted freedom for themselves and everyone who would come after them. These men knew they would be killed for treason if America lost the war, but they signed the Declaration of Independence anyway. They were telling the world that they were standing for liberty."

Caroline remained very quiet, wondering what Sergeant Joe was getting at.

"Well, we did win the war and the United States of America was born. Not long after, many of those same men wrote and signed the Constitution. It contains all the laws on which our nation is based. Our country was created through sacrifice, and many people throughout its history have given their lives to protect it and to protect the Constitution. They wanted their friends, their neighbors, their children and grandchildren, to live in a free and equal world."

"But why would they be willing to die for someone they didn't know?"

Sergeant Joe thought for a minute, "When you believe that everyone is created equal and that every man has worth, you are willing to die to make sure they will always be free. Even if you don't know them." Sergeant Joe patted Caroline on the head. She had to think about all of this. He cleared his throat, turned to the people on the shore and began to speak.

"My dear, dear friends, it fills my heart with gratitude to see you all here. We have each gained our freedom and our peace from the sacrifice of people we will never meet. We light these candles to remind ourselves of their love. We light them, hoping those men and women know they have not been forgotten."

The crowd was still and silent. Only the ocean moved and spoke. Sergeant Joe bowed his head and all the townspeople followed. Caroline did as well, but stole a peek or two.

Then, on cue, the lighthouse blazed its golden beam across the sea. That was the signal. Caroline helped her dad reach into their parcel and pull out a wax candle and a small cardboard boat. Soon every candle was lit, until the crowd looked like a trembling body of hovering stars.

In total silence, Caroline carefully lowered the candle into the little boat and then the boat into the water. Everyone watched as the little ships pitched to and fro on the first waves, heading out into the darkness of the night.

2 Introducing Good Deeds

Caroline saw Sergeant Joe place a tiny black and white photograph in his little boat, touch it gently and send it across the waves. She came up behind the old veteran and put her hand on his shoulder. He smiled up at her.

"Thank you for reminding us," she whispered.

The tiny, sparkling armada floated away, twinkling smaller and smaller. Eventually, they moved so far toward the horizon that the thin black line could hardly distinguish the lanterns from the stars. They floated and danced in Caroline's eyes as she wished her silent farewell.

Just the beginning...

Day 2   ART OF THE HEART®

1. The purpose of this activity is to assist your students in creating and signing an original Class Constitution, which should include the most important class rules that enable everyone to feel safe and to learn the most.

2. Remind your students that obeying the rules of our community and classroom shows RESPECT for those around us.

3. Ask your students to consider three things in creating the rules for the classroom: Words, Actions and Attitudes. Below are some examples, but encourage the students to create their own.

   ACTIONS   How should we behave ourselves at school?
   - Never hit or bully
   - Never run inside
   - Raise my hand when I want to speak
   - Leave a space cleaner than I found it

   WORDS   How should we speak to one another?
   - Always use kind words
   - Encourage one another
   - Use inside voice

   ATTITUDES   What attitudes in our heart should govern our words and actions?
   - Treat others the way I want to be treated
   - Listen respectfully to what my teacher says
   - Look for ways to help others

4. Write the student ideas for the Class Rules on the board as they brainstorm together. Limit the number of rules to 5-10 so that the students think carefully through what is most important.

5. Finalize the wording and sign on Day 4.

You'll Need:
- White Board
- Markers
- **Good Deeds** activity sheet (1/student)

Day 3   WRITING FROM THE HEART

Ask your students to consider the following journal prompt and answer it according to your classroom writing requirements: *Rules and laws are written for everyone's good. If you could write only one rule for the good of everyone in your classroom, what would it be? Tell why.*

You'll Need:
- **Introducing Good Deeds** activity sheet (1/student)

Days 2-5

Day 4 CREATIVE CONNECTION

1. Show your students the notes from the brainstorming session on Day 2.

2. As a class, decide the 5-10 rules that are most important to include in the Class Constitution.

3. Have your class copy the Class Constitution from the board and sign it.

4. Keep copies of the Constitution posted on the walls of the classroom for reference throughout the year.

5. Create a large version of the Class Constitution on poster board and have everyone put their "John Hancock" on it!

You'll Need:
- **Class Constitution** activity sheet
- Optional: poster board for large copy

Day 5 TECH TIME

Interactive Whiteboard Activity on MyManners Portal

Watch **Wilbur Goes to School!**

MANNERS IN ACTION

Whooooo will hang the **Happle** this week?

RESPECT—Treating others with dignity

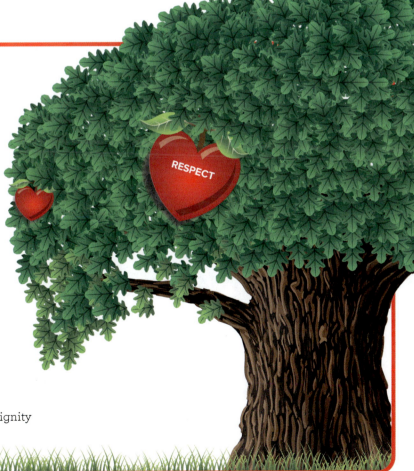

WEEK 3
CHOOSING RESPECT

Big Ideas

- Showing respect, especially in the face of disrespect, is always the right thing to do.

- A heart filled with the right stuff will produce respectful words and actions.

- Self-respect is the internal reward of offering respect to others.

For Your Heart

Think back to the movie classic, *Forrest Gump*. Have you ever considered the fact that Forrest gained the respect of everyone who ever knew him? Was it because he was "fast like the wind"? Or because he was a war hero? Or because he was a loyal friend?

Yes, yes, and yes, but even more. Forrest gave respect to everyone he met. He was respectful and respectable. He freely gave respect and lived in a way that gained respect.

Despite all he didn't know, he knew all he needed to know. He knew that giving respect was always the best thing to do, even when it was returned with disrespect. Giving respect without expectation of return, like Forrest did, isn't easy, but who ever said that doing the right thing is easy?

May we all be as smart as Forrest and choose respect!

For the Hearts of Your Students

You can prepare your students to successfully meet the challenges of life with a deeper understanding that giving respect is the first step in gaining respect, especially in the face of disrespect. Forrest Gump never returned the disrespect he was given, and with each incident of giving respect, his self-respect grew.

Children with self-respect are able to put others' needs ahead of their own. They begin to understand how their decisions directly affect those around them. Their confidence is balanced with humility, enabling them to develop the noble quality of humble confidence.

In this week's lesson, you have the privilege of cultivating *goodness* in the hearts of your students by giving them opportunities for *respect*. You'll help your students discover how good it feels on the inside to do the right thing, even when no one is looking.

Your students will begin the process of developing self-respect with each act of giving respect.

3 Choosing Respect

GOODNESS—Being kind, compassionate, and forgiving
RESPECT—Treating others with dignity

REMEMBER

SKILLS AND OBJECTIVES

- Children will learn that respect is an attitude of the heart.
- Children will learn that respectful words and actions show the good "seeds" in their hearts.
- Children will learn that good "seeds" grow with respectful words and deeds.

Wise Ol' Wilbur's Recommended Reading

Amos Fortune, Free Man by Elizabeth Yates

Despite his many hardships, Amos Fortune treated all people with respect. What does this show about his character?

GUIDING CHILDREN'S LEARNING

1. Introduce the definitions for this week's *Heart Attributes*: GOODNESS and RESPECT. Encourage your students to memorize and recite the definitions. They should also listen closely to the story for examples of both GOODNESS and RESPECT.

2. Let's Listen! Read aloud or play the recording of ***The Watchman of Merryville***.

3. After the story, lead your students in the following discussion questions:
   - *Who is Nicholas in the story?*
     A pirate who was shipwrecked during the storm.
   - *Why does Nicholas steal from the people of Merryville?*
     He lost everything at sea and stealing is the only life he has ever known.
   - *Do you think Ol' McDonald knew Nicholas was stealing? Why did he continue to help him?*
     Ol' McDonald probably knew he was stealing, but he also knew that kindness may help Nicholas' heart to grow.
   - *How did Nicholas' heart change?*
     He responded to Ol' McDonald's kindness. When he saw him hurt, he decided to help him.
   - *How do you know his heart changed?*
     He helped Ol' McDonald and he returned the stolen goods.

MANNERS IN ACTION

1. Point out the **Happle Tree** and how the number of **Happles** is growing. Remind your students that their hearts are growing as well!

2. Discuss these *Big Ideas* with your students:
   - *Showing RESPECT, especially in the face of disrespect, is always the right thing to do.*
   - *A heart filled with RESPECT will produce kind words and actions.*
   - *When we treat others with RESPECT, they will RESPECT us and we will grow in self-respect.*

3. Ask your children how they can show GOODNESS and RESPECT this week. Encourage them to name actions that demonstrate GOODNESS and to name people who deserve RESPECT. Challenge them to be the student who hangs a Happle at the end of the week!

Day 1

THE WATCHMAN OF MERRYVILLE

Once upon a heart in Merryville, a terrible storm gathered over the sea. Winds howled. Waves crashed. The sky became dark. Ol' Farmer McDonald knew this was a storm like no other he had ever seen. He jumped in his truck and headed to the lighthouse for a closer look.

When he got there, he saw a giant tornado roaring toward Merryville. Far from the shore, he could see a ship being tossed about in the waves. He rang the big brass bell, alerting the town folk to take cover.

Ol' McDonald jumped back in his truck and rushed to his farm to nail down his shutters. Folks along the way ran to safety. Bully and Buddy scurried down the road toward their home. Peter and Penelope started running, too!

Ol' McDonald was right. This was the worst storm to ever hit Merryville. Rain came down in buckets. Lightning lit up the sky!

Just after dark, Sketch peeked out from his tree trunk to see a tornado pass high in the sky, sparing Merryville. By morning, the sky was clear. Winds were calm. Birds were singing. The sun shone brightly. Wilbur, the wise old owl, came out of his Happle Tree and called out, "Whooooo, Weee, what a night!"

Townspeople came out to check on their neighbors. Everyone seemed to be alright, but Merryville was a mess. Ol' McDonald wondered about the ship he had seen during the storm and who might have been on it.

Wilbur flew down to check on his friend when he saw someone go into McDonald's barn. "Whooooo goes there?" Wilbur called.

Ol' McDonald was startled and headed to the barn. There, he saw a barefoot young man, soaking wet like he just climbed out of the sea. He had a black scarf on his head, an earring in his ear, and an old key tied around his neck. When the young man heard Wilbur, he hid his sack full of stolen loot behind a stack of hay bales. Ol' McDonald knew this young man must be a pirate from the ship at sea.

"You look like you could use a hot meal. Would you like to join me for breakfast?" asked Ol' McDonald. Without a smile or a thank you, the young man nodded.

This was the first time in this young pirate's life anyone had been so kind. He told Ol' McDonald his name was Nicholas and that he paddled to shore in a life raft just before the ship sank.

Ol' McDonald never asked Nicholas why he was in his barn, but offered him dry clothes and a pair of shoes. The young man changed his clothes, put on his new shoes, then headed back toward town, still without thanking Ol' McDonald.

There was plenty of work in town after the storm. Nicholas worked for different folks during the day and came back to steal from them at night.

After awhile, Nicholas knew he better move on or he would get caught. He heard the train blow its whistle and knew this was his only escape. He threw his bag of loot on top of feed sacks in the back of Ol' McDonald's truck and headed for the station. Just as he drove past the bean field, Nicholas heard Chester barking like a crazy dog. He looked over to see Chester standing next to Ol' McDonald who was lying by the road.

Nicholas knew if he stopped to help him, he would miss the train. But something strange was happening in Nicholas' heart. For the first time in his life, Nicholas thought about someone other than himself. He slammed on the brakes and ran to Ol' McDonald who had a big knot on the side of his head.

Nicholas put Ol' McDonald in the truck and drove straight to Dr. Feltbetter's office. Ol' McDonald's head was okay, but his right arm was broken and had to be put in a cast.

When Dr. Feltbetter finished wrapping Ol' McDonald's arm, Nicholas took him back to the farm and tucked him in bed. He sat next to his bed all night long. The next morning, he fed the kind old man breakfast and started doing chores around the farm. With each kindness, his heart began to grow.

At night, he started returning the stolen goods. Every time he took something back, his heart grew more. Soon, he found himself wanting to help others, rather than hurt them.

After breakfast, he took a deep breath and told Ol' McDonald the truth.

"When I was in the storm at sea," Nicholas said, "my treasure chest full of gold washed overboard. I came into Merryville to steal as much as I had lost. The day you found me in your barn, I was stealing from you, but you were kind to me. You gave me food and clothing. You taught me that giving is better than taking. For the first time in my life, I felt a part of something good. All I want to do with the rest of my life is help others like you helped me."

"I know just the job for you," answered Ol' McDonald. They headed into town to see the Mayor of Merryville who agreed Nicholas was the right man to watch over Merryville.

The very next day, the town folk gathered at the lighthouse as the Mayor gave Nicholas the key to the lighthouse and

3 Choosing Respect

his new title, "Cap'n Nick, the Watchman of Merryville."
   To this day, he lives in the lighthouse by the sea and watches over Merryville by day and by night.

Just the beginning...

Day 2   ART OF THE HEART®

1. Give each student an activity sheet.

2. Have students write three different "good seed" words or phrases on the "Seeds of Respect".

3. Have students cut out the seeds and the seed packet.

4. Next, ask them to fold the flap on the long side of the seed packet first and run a bit of glue down it. Fold the back piece over and glue in place on top of the flap. Fold the bottom flap up and glue in place to make the packet.

5. Invite your students to draw a picture of their favorite fruit on the front.

6. Set aside the Seed Packets for discussion on Day 4.

You'll Need:
- **Seeds of Respect** activity sheets (1/student)
- Scissors
- Glue
- Colored pencils

Day 3   WRITING FROM THE HEART

Ask your students to consider the following journal prompt and answer it according to your classroom writing requirements:

Describe a time that you saw someone being bullied or treated with disrespect. How did it make you feel?

You'll Need:
- **Choosing Respect** activity sheet (1/student)

Days 2-5

Day 4 CREATIVE CONNECTION

1. Begin the lesson by asking the following questions:
   - *Do you think it matters what kinds of seeds you plant in a garden?*
   Yes, you want to plant the seeds for the kinds of fruits or flowers you want to grow.
   - *Can you produce good fruit if the seeds you use are not good?*
   No, good fruit only comes from good seeds.
   - *In the same way, good words and actions grow from good seeds in your heart. In the same way weeds prevent good seeds from growing in a garden, anger and selfishness prevent good things from growing in your heart. Does a person with anger in his heart usually act kindly toward others?*
   No, we usually do what our heart feels.
   - *Today, we want to talk about the good seeds of respectfulness. What are some good things we can say and do to plant "good seeds" of respect in the hearts of others?*
   Say: "I love you", "Please", "Thank you", "Excuse me", "I'm sorry", "Can I help you?"
   Do: Help someone clean up their mess, hold the door open for others, smile, let someone else go first, wait our turn

2. Invite your students to share which "seeds" they chose to put in their packets and why. Encourage students throughout the year to remember to plant good seeds of RESPECT.

You'll Need:
- **Seeds of Respect** packets from Day 2
- Scissors
- Glue
- Colored pencils

Day 5 TECH TIME

Interactive Whiteboard Activity on MyManners Portal

Who knew growing a plant could be this tough?!

MANNERS IN ACTION

Whooooo will hang the **Happle** this week?

GOODNESS—Being kind, compassionate, and forgiving
RESPECT—Treating others with dignity

WEEK 4
HELPING OTHERS

Big Ideas

• When children begin to put the needs of others ahead of their own wants, their hearts begin to grow. As their hearts grow, their minds will open.

• Acts of kindness and love help children develop others-centeredness, which enables them to become valuable members of their community.

• Helping others makes the world a better place.

For Your Heart

We all know and love the children's classic, *How the Grinch Stole Christmas*. The Grinch spent his days concocting a dastardly scheme to ruin Christmas for the Whos. Dr. Seuss gave the most out-of-the-ordinary reason for why the Grinch hated Christmas so much:

> *It could be his head wasn't screwed on just right.*
> *It could be, perhaps, that his shoes were too tight.*
> ***But I think that the most likely reason of all***
> ***May have been that his heart was two sizes too small.***

At Manners of the Heart, we believe this is the reason for the Grinch's struggles as it is for many of us. His heart was scarred and locked from old wounds. Whether someone is unkind, selfish, entitled, broken, impoverished, overindulged or disrespectful, the cure is the same. Seeing the wounded hearts of your students and nurturing them with kindness, love and respect is the greatest privilege you are given as a teacher.

For the Hearts of Your Students

The answer to your students' struggles is to unlock their hearts, which will open their minds to the knowledge you have for them. With the first turn of the key, they experience the joy of helping others.

After the Grinch had stolen Christmas from the Whos in Whoville, he heard singing instead of crying!

> *And what happened then? Well in Whoville they say*
> ***That the Grinch's small heart grew three sizes that day.***

In an instant, the Grinch's heart began filling with *kindness* and *love*, and he returned Christmas to the Whos. His outward expressions of kindness reflected the inward condition of the love growing in his heart.

In this week's lesson, you'll be teaching your students what it means to help others. They will experience the excitement of a growing heart and a mind opening to receive the knowledge you have to share.

4 Helping Others

KINDNESS—Showing care for others in an unexpected and exceptional way

LOVE—Genuinely caring for others

REMEMBER

SKILLS AND OBJECTIVES

- Children will learn to look for ways to help others.
- Children will learn to show kindness in tangible ways.
- Children will learn to demonstrate kindness from a heart of love.

Wise Ol' Wilbur's Recommended Reading

Sarah, Plain and Tall
by Patricia MacLachlin

Can you identify examples of Sarah showing kindness and love to other characters?

GUIDING CHILDREN'S LEARNING

1. Introduce the definitions for this week's *Heart Attributes*: KINDNESS and LOVE. Encourage your students to memorize and recite the definitions. They should also listen closely to the story for examples of both *Heart Attributes*.

2. Let's Listen! Read aloud or play the recording of ***I'll Help You and You'll Help Me.***

3. After the story, lead your students in the following discussion questions:
    - *Who can sing?*
      Brianna
    - *Who can play basketball?*
      Jerome
    - *Who is great at math?*
      Trey
    - *Mrs. Sweetwater noticed a problem in her class. What was it?*
      Everyone was so worried about the things they couldn't do, that they forgot what they could do!
    - *What was Mrs. Sweetwater's solution?*
      She asked everyone to help someone else with a skill they knew how to do well.
    - *What things do you do well? In which skills do you struggle?* (Answers will vary)
    - *How does it feel to help someone else? How does it feel to be helped?* (Answers will vary)

MANNERS IN ACTION

1. Point out the **Happle Tree** and how the number of Happles is growing. Remind your students that their hearts are growing as well!

2. Discuss these *Big Ideas* with your students:
    - Everyone is good at something, but no one is good at everything!
    - There are opportunities to help others all around us.
    - Helping others comes from a heart of LOVE.

3. Ask your children how they can show KINDNESS and LOVE this week. Encourage students to look for opportunities to give an act of KINDNESS at school or at home and to offer help from a heart of LOVE. Challenge them to be the student who hangs a Happle at the end of the week!

Day 1

I'LL HELP YOU, AND YOU'LL HELP ME

Once upon a heart in Merryville, Tommy and his friends were fourth graders at Merryville Elementary School. As the school year moved on, they began to notice that not everyone was good at everything.

Jasmine was an amazing artist, but she wasn't good at any game that used a ball. Wesley, on the other hand, couldn't draw anything recognizable, but he knew the difference between a cell and an organ in science class.

Brianna loved to sing, but couldn't write a good story because she wasn't very good at grammar. Now, Caroline couldn't sing at all, but she could read a book a day and remember what she read.

Tommy knew how to catch all kinds of fish in Mirror Lake, but he was not very interested in reading and was always falling behind in his assignments. Believe it or not, Jerome couldn't bait his own hook, but he could out-dribble anyone during basketball practice.

Trey could add, subtract, multiply and divide in his head, which was a good thing, because he couldn't keep up with his notebook and pencil. Poor Jack couldn't add two plus two, but he understood how to write a sentence better than almost anyone.

It turned out that everybody was good at something, but no one was good at everything.

It wasn't long before everyone was paying more attention to what they couldn't do, than what they could do. Jasmine stopped drawing her beautiful pictures, because she spent all her time wishing she was good at sports like Jerome.

Jack worried so much about being good in math like Trey, that he fell behind on his writing assignments.

Jerome just quit fishing altogether with his friends, because he got tired of trying to bait the hook with his great big hands.

Caroline became so obsessed with wanting to sing as well as Brianna, that she stopped going to the library for new books to read and just sat around doing nothing.

As the school year went on, Mrs. Sweetwater noticed her students were complaining a lot and not getting their work done as well as they had at the beginning of the school year. The more she watched, the more she began to understand the problem. After a few days, Mrs. Sweetwater knew what to do.

"Students, starting today, we're going to turn things upside down in our class. At different times this week, I want each of you to find someone who needs help learning to do what you can do. Trey, you can help Jack work on his multiplication tables. Jack, you can teach Brianna how to construct a good sentence. Brianna, you can help Caroline learn a new song. And Caroline, you can help Tommy learn how to enjoy reading the way you do, so he can finish assignments on time. You see, class we all have something we can teach someone else and something we can learn from someone else. That's what makes a good team. Not competing but cooperating."

It didn't take long for Mrs. Sweetwater's idea to catch on. By the end of the week, no one was worrying about what they couldn't do anymore. They were too busy teaching each other new skills. And guess what happened?

It turned out that everyone learned something new and got even better at what they already knew how to do well!

Just the beginning...

4 Helping Others

Day 2 MUSIC OF THE HEART®

1. Read or watch "The Grinch Who Stole Christmas" as a class.
2. Lead your class in discussion, using the following questions as a guide.
   - *Why did the Grinch want to steal the Whos' Christmas?*
     His heart was "two sizes too small."
   - *How do the Whos react when the Grinch steals their presents?*
     They start singing even though everything is gone, because they know the true meaning of Christmas.
   - *What happens to the Grinch's heart when he hears the Whos singing?*
     His heart grows "three sizes that day."
     His heart gets so big, he doesn't think about himself any longer. He thinks only of how he can help the Whos.

You'll Need:
- *The Grinch Who Stole Christmas* by Dr. Seuss book or original movie

Day 3 WRITING FROM THE HEART

Ask your students to consider the following journal prompt and answer it according to your classroom writing requirements:

Think about someone outside your family who helps you. Describe who they are and what they do to help you. Why do you think they choose to help you?

You'll Need:
- **Helping Others** activity sheet (1/student)

Days 2-5

Day 4 CREATIVE CONNECTION

1. Give each student an activity sheet.

2. Ask students to think of the people around them who help them. Encourage them to think of those at home, at school, at church, etc.

3. As students fill in the first two columns, ask them to think of ways they can help those who help them.

4. Encourage your students to tell the class about one of the special people they have described.

You'll Need:
- Helping You and Me activity sheet (1/student)
- Pencils

Day 5 TECH TIME

Interactive Whiteboard Activity on MyManners Portal

Can you set a record cleaning up this room?!

MANNERS IN ACTION

Whooooo will hang the **Happle** this week?

KINDNESS—Showing care for others in an unexpected and exceptional way
LOVE—Genuinely caring for others

WEEK 5
FORGIVING OTHERS

Big Ideas

- A child with a patient and humble heart will be able to both give and receive forgiveness.

- Until they learn patience in excusing the faults of others, children have great difficulty maturing socially and emotionally.

- Humility is cultivated in the heart of a child who learns to ask to be forgiven when at fault.

For Your Heart

Clara Barton, founder of the American Red Cross, was reminded one day of a hurtful deed someone had done to her years before. She acted as if she had never even heard of the incident. "Don't you remember it?" her friend asked. "No," came Barton's reply, "I distinctly remember forgetting it."

What a beautiful example Clara Barton gives us of excusing others. She gives deeper meaning to the old adage of "forgive and forget".

Too often, we are quick to judge the behaviors of others, yet slow to recognize our own faults. An important aspect of getting along with others involves learning how to excuse the faults of others while recognizing our faults and asking others to excuse them.

Being slow to take offense and quick to offer forgiveness enables us to be part of fostering respect and civility in our school culture.

For the Hearts of Your Students

You can help your students develop the ability to excuse others by giving them opportunities to practice patience with their fellow classmates. In *The Turtle and the Skunk*, Sketch learns a hard lesson in patience when he leaves Henry in the dust and becomes lost himself!

In this week's lesson, you will help your students cultivate the ability to forgive and to ask to be forgiven. By forgiving and excusing others, they develop *patience* in accepting the shortcomings of others. By asking to be forgiven when they wrong a fellow student, they learn *humility*, a quality that is much more about how we treat others than what we think of ourselves.

5 Forgiving Others

PATIENCE—Even-tempered endurance

HUMILITY—Not caring who gets credit

REMEMBER

SKILLS AND OBJECTIVES

- Children will learn that it is important to forgive others, even when they have not asked for it.
- Children will learn that forgiveness is good for us, and it is good for the other people in our lives.

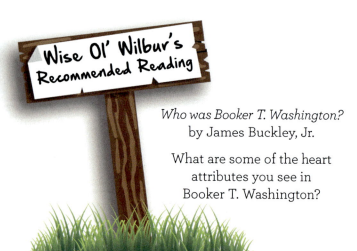

Who was Booker T. Washington? by James Buckley, Jr.

What are some of the heart attributes you see in Booker T. Washington?

GUIDING CHILDREN'S LEARNING

1. Introduce the *Heart Attributes* and definitions for this week: PATIENCE and HUMILITY.
2. Read or listen to this week's story, **Forgiven**. Do you hear illustrations of the *Heart Attributes*?
3. Discussion questions:
    - *Tommy shared a secret with Jasmine. What did Jasmine do with that secret?*
      She shared it with others and it became gossip.
    - *How do we know that Tommy found out what Jasmine had done?*
      He was crying the next day in class.
    - *How do you think Tommy felt?*
      Betrayed, embarrassed
    - *Who did Jasmine see after school that day?*
      Florence the Flower Lady
    - *Jasmine destroyed some of Florence's flowers. How did Florence react?*
      She forgave Jasmine. She comforted and hugged her.
    - *What else did Jasmine need forgiveness for?*
      Jasmine had betrayed Tommy.
    - *Who best showed PATIENCE and HUMILITY in* **Forgiven***?*
      Florence the Flower Lady

MANNERS IN ACTION

1. In **Forgiven**, we see Florence the Flower Lady showing Jasmine the healing nature of forgiveness.
2. Discuss these *Big Ideas*:
    - *It is important to forgive others even if they have not apologized or asked forgiveness.*
    - *Forgiveness is good for others.*
    - *Forgiveness is good for us, too.*
3. Challenge your students to show forgiveness to others this week, even when they have not asked for it. *Look for PATIENCE and HUMILITY in one another and share stories of what you have seen on Day 5.*

Day 1

FORGIVEN

Once upon a heart in Merryville, Tommy whispered in Jasmine's ear, "I have a secret, but you have to promise not to tell anyone."

Jasmine's heart skipped a beat. She nodded solemnly and leaned in to listen to what Tommy had to say. He cupped his hands around his mouth.

Jasmine held her breath so she could hear every word. All the other kids at school were running around the playground during recess. She felt kind of special knowing something none of them knew.

"I like Sarah," Tommy whispered.

Jasmine gasped and put her hand over her mouth, "You mean you like, *like* Sarah?" Tommy nodded with a big silly grin on his face.

Jasmine mouthed the words wow and yeah, but inside her chest she felt a little, burning sting. She didn't know exactly why, but Tommy's secret kind of hurt.

"Don't tell anyone!" Tommy demanded, then ran off to play and motioned for Jasmine to join him.

Jasmine didn't feel like it. She saw a group of her friends sitting in a little clump, giggling. She knew exactly what she felt like doing…

"Hey, Sarah! You'll never guess what Tommy just told me."

* * *

The next day, Jasmine had an ice-cold, hollow feeling in the deepest part of her stomach. She tried to ignore it, but it froze there. The feeling grew worse when she saw Tommy walk into class. He was hanging his head with his hair covering his eyes.

"Tommy!" Jasmine whispered as loudly as she dared.

She could hear Sarah and some of their friends laughing away in the back of the class.

"Tommy!" Jasmine whispered again.

For just a moment, Tommy tilted his head sideways to see her. Jasmine could see two tears trickling down the end of his nose. The feeling in her stomach grew worse.

After school, Jasmine shuffled along the sidewalk, kicking at the curb. *Ding. Ding. Ding-a-ling!* Jasmine heard a cheerful little bell.

"Yoohoooo," called a beautiful voice as soft and ripply as the spring that tumbles down Merryville Mountain. Jasmine recognized it at once.

"Miss Florence! I thought that was you."

Florence the Flower Lady pulled her bright green bicycle to a halt. Attached to the handlebars and mounted over the front wheel was a faded wooden cart brimming with flowers tucked in tiny pots and baskets. The cart was so big that the bike looked almost small in comparison. Ruby carnations, pink tulips, flimsy irises and fiery lilies all jostled each other in the wind for a glimpse of the sun or their driver's gentle smile.

Florence was the kind of lady who seemed like she had never known a sad day. She could find something beautiful in everything - in the tiniest weed or the oldest, most gnarled tree. She'd gaze on it, smile with only the left side of her mouth and pet the hair that was always peeking from behind her ears back into its flower-shaped pins. It was then, you knew she was admiring something beautiful.

Looking at Jasmine with great empathy, Miss Florence said, "You're wilted."

Jasmine couldn't help but smile, "Tough day."

The Flower Lady's eyes softened, "I'm no stranger to those. I'm sorry," Florence answered.

"It's nothing," Jasmine shrugged.

"By the tone of your voice, sounds like it's something, not nothing." Florence fixed her hair, but it popped back out almost before she was done. "You know what? Can you watch my flowers for me?"

Florence trotted off toward Charlotte's Chocolate Shoppe. Jasmine didn't know why, but as she stood there waiting, her face flushed with anger. *She doesn't understand. Florence has never felt this bad.* Without thinking, she took a few of the tulips between her thumbnail and her index finger and slit the stem. The flowers were no match for that. Leaking out water, the bright green stems gave way and split open. Jasmine even flicked a few of the jewel-like petals into the wind and watched them with satisfaction as they floated to the pavement. But the satisfaction didn't last long.

"Jasmine! Why?" Florence stood behind her, a small basket of chilled, chocolate-covered strawberries in her hands. Her eyes were full of loss as she looked at the crushed flowers.

5 Forgiving Others

Then, she did something that surprised Jasmine very much. She rested the strawberries on the back of the cart, cradled Jasmine's head between her hands and drew the little girl in for a hug. Before she knew what was happening, Jasmine felt hot streams of tears running down her cheeks and soaking into Florence's floral sundress. An image floated into Jasmine's mind, as she stood there, enveloped in the Flower Lady's arms. *I wonder if this is how the flowers feel when Florence plants them and pats the soft, dark earth around them.*

"I'm sorry. I'm so sorry, Florence," Jasmine mumbled through her tears.

Florence leaned back, wiped Jasmine's eyes with her thumbs and gazed deeply at the little girl.

"Beautiful things are easy to destroy, even though they take a long time to grow. What's going on, Jasmine?"

"I did a terrible thing at school." Jasmine felt a weight lift from her shoulders.

"Did you apologize?"

"I tried right after school, but Tommy didn't want to talk."

"Sometimes beautiful things take a long time to grow back, too."

"I can't take back what I said, Florence. I wish I could."

Florence peered into the basket of crumpled flowers on the cart. Beneath the ruins was an untouched tulip. Gingerly, Florence lifted it up and placed it in a small vase. "Here, Jasmine," she said as she held it out to the sniffling little girl.

"I can pay for them," Jasmine offered.

"Oh, no," Florence cooed, "Everything's forgiven. Just take care of this little flower."

"I don't think I..."

"Shhh," Florence hushed, "Each little flower knows it is beautiful long before you do. All it asks is that you see it, and take care of it. You should see yourself through my eyes, Jasmine. Beautiful and wholly forgiven."

Jasmine's eyes floated down to the tulip. It really was beautiful there with the sun seeping through its petals. *I think I see what Florence sees,* she mused to herself.

Just the beginning...

Day 2   ART OF THE HEART®

1. Begin by asking students to think about how they feel when someone hurts their feelings. Choose several students to draw a face on the board showing how they feel.

2. Lead students in this discussion:
   - *Sometimes people ask for our forgiveness and this helps us feel better. What is the right thing to do when someone asks for forgiveness?*
     Say "I forgive you" and mean it.
     Don't bring up the mistake again – to the person or to someone else.
     Give him/her a hug to show you've forgiven him.
   - *When people do not ask for forgiveness, should we forgive them anyway? Why or why not?*
     Forgiveness helps the person who hurt you.
     Forgiveness helps us let go of anger, sadness and frustration.
     When we don't forgive, it is much harder to trust others in the future.
     Keeping bad feelings inside is much worse for us than for the person who hurt us.
     Remind children that forgiveness does not mean they must put themselves in a situation where they may be hurt again by the same person. For example, if a friend shares their secret with others, they should forgive him or her, but they can choose not to tell that person private information in the future.

You'll Need:
- Whiteboard
- Markers

Days 2-5

Day 3 WRITING FROM THE HEART

You'll Need:
- Paper and pencil

1. Have students write a letter of forgiveness to someone who has hurt them in the past. Explain that this letter is not meant to be shared with the person in real life, but that writing their thoughts and feelings down will help the students be able to forgive that person in their heart so they won't be angry anymore.
2. After writing the letter, fold it carefully. Allow your students to tear up the letters and put them in a garbage can. Remind your students that forgiving others, even when they have not asked for our forgiveness, is good for us and good for the other people in our lives.

Day 4 CREATIVE CONNECTION

You'll Need:
- My Forgiveness Pledge activity sheet (1/student)
- Pencils

1. Give each student a copy of **My Forgiveness Pledge** activity sheet.
2. Read the pledge aloud as a class and discuss what forgiveness truly means.
3. If students are willing and ready to make the promise, sign and date the bottom.
4. Tell them to show their pledge to a friend or family member who can help them remember to forgive others in the future.
5. Draw a face on the bottom that shows how we feel when we forgive others.

Day 5 TECH TIME

Interactive Whiteboard Activity on MyManners Portal

Solve the maze to help Sketch make his way back to his friend.

MANNERS IN ACTION

Whooooo will hang the **Happle** this week?

PATIENCE—Even-tempered endurance
HUMILITY—Not caring who gets credit

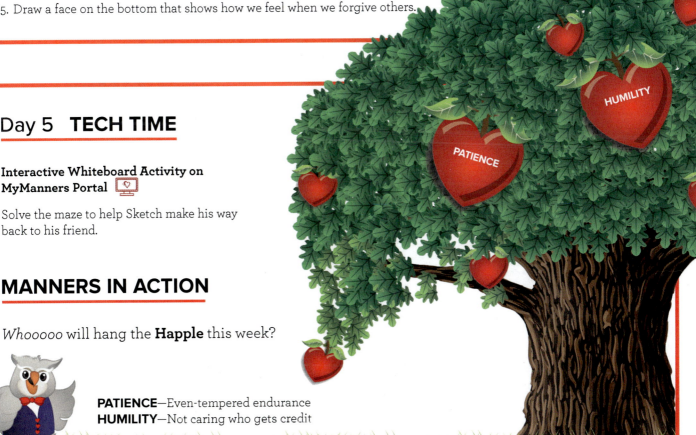

WEEK 6
APPRECIATING OTHERS

Big Ideas

- Learning to show appreciation for others through kind words and selfless deeds develops others-centeredness in children's hearts.

- Children who receive words of encouragement and appreciation feel valued.

- Children who learn to freely give compliments to others will become adults who add great value to our world.

For Your Heart

A survey of 2,000 Americans from all walks of life revealed that while 50% of people express appreciation to their immediate family on a daily basis, only 15% of people do so with their colleagues. And yet, nearly 90% of the survey respondents expressed a strong desire to have their coworkers say "Thank you" *to them* more often!

Just imagine for a moment if you set a goal of giving three compliments—kind words of appreciation and encouragement—to your fellow teachers and coworkers every day. Let's tweak the Golden Rule and compliment others the way we want to be complimented!

This simple practice could transform the culture of your school from one of discouragement to one of encouragement where the impossible becomes possible. Morale would be boosted, and enthusiasm for teaching would escalate. Your students would gain a different perspective on life, equipping them to turn our upside-down world right-side-up again!

Jim Stovall, author of *The Ultimate Gift*, reminds us that we "need to be aware of what others are doing, applaud their efforts, acknowledge their successes, and encourage them in their pursuits. When we all help one another, everybody wins."

For the Hearts of Your Students

When you appreciate and encourage your fellow teachers and your students encourage and appreciate each other, a learning environment of high achievement is created.

In this week's lesson, you'll help your students experience the great joy that comes from offering *encouragement* to others through kind words, generous actions and thoughtful deeds. Helping your students develop *appreciation* and acknowledge the accomplishments of their classmates creates a spirit of cooperation in your classroom.

6 Appreciating Others

ENCOURAGEMENT—Offering words to others to build their confidence

APPRECIATION—Recognizing and acknowledging value in people, places and things

REMEMBER

SKILLS AND OBJECTIVES

- Children will learn how to offer words of affirmation to others.
- Children will learn that the more you give away, the more you have.

Somebody Loves You, Mr. Hatch
by Eileen Spinelli

What changes do you see in Mr. Hatch when he believes somebody loves him?

GUIDING CHILDREN'S LEARNING

In today's story, students will begin to understand the importance of appreciating others, and how this shows respect.

1. Introduce this week's *Heart Attributes*: APPRECIATION and ENCOURAGEMENT
2. Review and discuss the *Heart Attributes* daily. Encourage children to memorize and review the definitions.
3. It's Story Time! Read aloud or play the recording of **Tommy's Treasure.**
4. After the story, lead your children in a discussion with the following questions:
   - *What advice did Terrell give Tommy about the treasure he had found?*
   He should give the coins away to others who didn't have any money, like Cap'n Nick.
   - *What happens to Tommy when he is selfish with the coins he finds?*
   He grows lonely and sad.
   - *What happens to Tommy when he begins giving the coins away?*
   His heart is touched and he wants to give away more.
   - *What did Tommy APPRECIATE more, his treasure, or the people of Merryville? How do you know?*
   Tommy appreciated the people of Merryville more because he gave away his treasure to help them and cheer them up.
   - *Have you ever gotten to share something special – things or words – with another person?* (Answers will vary)

MANNERS IN ACTION

1. As you wrap up the discussion of the story with the students, review the definitions of APPRECIATION and ENCOURAGEMENT.
2. Discuss these *Big Ideas* with your students:
   - *Affirming others is a way to show them how much you APPRECIATE them.*
   - *When we affirm others, it ENCOURAGES them.*
   - *The more you give away, the more you have.*
3. Ask your students to think of very specific things they can say to someone this week to encourage them. As they think about family members and peers at school, challenge them to look for opportunities to show APPRECIATION and ENCOURAGEMENT. At the end of the week, let the children tell their stories of how others reacted when they encouraged them.

Day 1

TOMMY'S TREASURE

Once upon a heart in Merryville, Tommy Tripper went for a walk along the beach looking for treasure. It was one of his favorite things to do when he felt lonely. Day after day, he collected seashells and shark teeth, starfish and sand dollars. Until one day, the bright sunlight revealed a shiny gold coin in the sand. He looked around to see if anyone was watching. There was no one in sight, so he reached down and picked it up.

The coin looked to be old, much older than he. When he looked at the face on the coin, it appeared the face on the coin looked back at him. Tommy's heart began to pound as his mind raced with possibilities. Where did the coin come from? Could there be more coins buried in the sand? What if there's a treasure chest nearby filled with gold coins?

The sun began to set. Tommy held the coin tightly in his hand and headed home, telling no one about his discovery. He tossed and turned all night. He couldn't stop thinking about all that awaited him the next morning.

The sun was barely up when he left the breakfast table and headed to the beach to look for more treasure. Today was even better than yesterday. Everywhere he looked, he found another coin and another and another. That night, he hid his coins in the back of his closet.

Again, he tossed and turned all night. He couldn't wait to go back to the beach, but this time he would go prepared. He would bring his book bag, so he could keep his coins safe.

During the night, a storm blew in, bringing an extra high tide. The surf washed all kinds of stuff up on the sand—seaweed and bottles, old boots and cans. The more Tommy searched, the more junk he found, until he saw a flash of light in the surf. He combed through the sand to find another coin. When he reached down for the coin, he stumped his toe on a small wooden box. Knowing it was something special, he picked it up and carried it back to the beach.

Tommy put the box down and looked back at the waves. He noticed a trail of coins behind him. He walked back to pick up the coins and, one by one, put them in his pockets. Tommy made sure no one was around and knelt in front of the old box.

Hanging on the front of the box was a rusty lock that broke in his hands when he touched it. Tommy felt his heart skip a beat with excitement over the mystery of the box. His hands trembled as he lifted the lid to reveal a box full of gold coins! A treasure chest! Tommy had never seen such a sight. Scared that someone might find it, he put the chest in his book bag. He ran home as fast as he could to put it in a secret hiding place in his backyard.

For days, he played with his new treasure. He built a tower with his coins, but the wind blew it down. He dug a hole and buried his treasure like the pirates of old, but his dog dug them up.

He went back to the beach and built a sand castle of coins, but the tide washed it away. He put some coins in his pocket, but he had a hole in his pocket. Instead of playing with friends, he counted the coins. He didn't tell anyone about his great treasure, because he was afraid they would take it from him.

After weeks of hiding his treasure, Tommy was so lonely, he decided he had to share his secret with his best friend, Terrell. His best buddy couldn't believe his eyes when he saw the chest full of gold coins hidden behind Tommy's clubhouse. "How much money is in this chest?" Terrell asked, as he sifted coins through his fingers. Tommy fell back in the grass and stared at clouds floating in the sky. "More money than I can ever spend," he answered.

"Tommy, you know the old sea captain who lives at the end of the road in the lighthouse?" Terrell asked with excitement in his voice. "Everybody knows Cap'n Nick," replied Tommy. "He watches the sea to protect Merryville from storms."

"Did you know he hardly has enough money to feed himself?' asked Jack. "Why don't you share some of your gold coins with him? He could sure use the help."

Tommy and Terrell put a few coins in a bag and left them on Cap'n Nick's doorstep with a note that said, "From your friend." They knocked on the door, then hid in the bushes and watched the old sea captain find his gift. Cap'n Nick smiled, looked around, then looked up for a moment, before he grabbed his jacket and headed to town.

Watching Cap'n Nick's happiness gave Tommy great joy in his heart. From that day on, Tommy looked for people in Merryville who needed help. He gave sacks of coins to other boys and girls, moms and dads, old folks and poor folks and more. Tommy never felt lonely again. The smile on his face showed the warmth in his heart.

Are you wondering how long Tommy's treasure lasted? Forever and ever. For you see, the more love Tommy gave away, the more love he had to give.

Just the beginning...

6 Appreciating Others

Day 2 ART OF THE HEART®

1. Distribute the activity sheets.

2. Have students color the hearts yellow or gold on one side and cut them out.

3. Have them write words of ENCOURAGEMENT on the opposite side.
   Some examples:
   - I like you!
   - Thank you!
   - You're doing a great job!
   - Wow, you're fast! (or smart! or strong!)
   - You have a nice smile!

4. Color and cut out the treasure chest. Fold on the dotted lines to make a pocket that will hold the hearts of gold.

5. Staple the edges of the chest closed. Give your students the opportunity to pass the hearts of gold to their neighbors to offer a kind word of APPRECIATION or ENCOURAGEMENT.

You'll Need:
- **My Treasure Chest** activity sheet (1/student)
- **Hearts of Gold** activity sheet (1/student)
- Scissors
- Crayons or colored pencils
- Stapler

Day 3 WRITING FROM THE HEART

Ask your students to consider the following journal prompt and answer it according to your classroom writing requirements:

Think about someone in your family and describe three things you appreciate about them.

You'll Need:
- **Appreciating Others** activity sheet (1/student)

Days 2-5

Day 4   CREATIVE CONNECTION

1. Remind your students of their **Treasure Chests of Gold** and then lead them in this discussion:
    - *What are some treasures that don't cost any money, which you can give away to make others happy?*
    Telling others to, "Have a nice day!"
    Saying, "Good job!"
    Letting others go first
    Saying, "I love you"
    Smiling

2. Gather your students in a large circle. Instruct one student to throw the ball to another with a "treasure" or compliment. The one who receives the ball then throws it to another, giving another compliment, and so on. Encourage the students to throw the ball to someone new each time so that everyone receives a word of ENCOURAGEMENT.

3. Close the lesson by coaching your students on showing APPRECIATION for the cafeteria staff. Suggest phrases they can use as they're leaving the line:
    - Thank you for serving us.
    - Have a nice day!

4. Remind students that one of the reasons they're to pick up after themselves is to make the job of the staff easier and show APPRECIATION for the work they do.

You'll Need:
- Ball

Day 5   TECH TIME

Interactive Whiteboard Activity on MyManners Portal

Check out this fun video to see how colorful kindness can be.

MANNERS IN ACTION

Whooooo will hang the **Happle** this week?

ENCOURAGEMENT—Offering words to others to build their confidence
APPRECIATION—Recognizing and acknowledging value in people, places and things

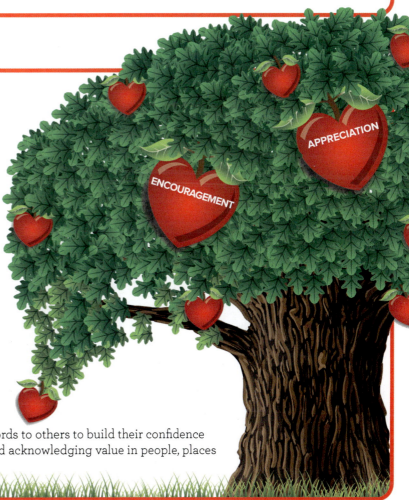

WEEK 7
BEING A BUDDY, NOT A BULLY

Big Ideas

- Children demonstrate kindness for others when they care about the feelings of others.
- Children find acceptance when their hearts are opened by kindness.
- Children learn how much better it is to be a buddy, than to be a bully.

For Your Heart

The actions of an elementary age child who pushes his classmates around are coming from a troubled heart—a heart filled with anger and disappointment. A heart locked for self-protection. From one end of the spectrum to the other, too many of today's children are growing up without their heart needs being met, which always results in trouble on the outside.

Bullies are in desperate need of acceptance. The chances are great they are suffering from one of three difficult scenarios in their upbringing:

- They are being indulged without discipline
- They are being disciplined harshly
- They are being exposed to too much, too soon

The results are the same. They struggle with their identity. They struggle with anger and heartache. They struggle to find a place where they belong, and yet build walls around them to keep others out.

Your classroom can be the place where they find acceptance and understanding.

For the Hearts of Your Students

When elementary school children were asked why kids bully, they said, "Their hearts are full of the wrong stuff." The children know the truth, don't they?

In this week's lesson, you have the honor of filling the hearts of your students with the right stuff. You will be helping them replace the wrong stuff with the right stuff—*kindness* and *acceptance*.

You can help your students experience the joy of making a difference in another person's life by treating others with kindness and acceptance, rather than disapproval and rejection. It's amazing how quickly a child's behavior can be transformed when he is accepted where he is with the great anticipation and expectation of becoming more than he is today.

We all need someone to believe in us and help us reach our full potential.

7 Being a Buddy, Not a Bully

ACCEPTANCE—Treating everyone you meet with the same respect, regardless of differences

KINDNESS—Showing care for others in an unexpected and exceptional way

REMEMBER

SKILLS AND OBJECTIVES

- Children will learn why it is important to stand up for someone who is being bullied.
- Children will learn what actions to take when they witness bullying.
- Children will learn how to help a bully become a buddy.

Wise Ol' Wilbur's Recommended Reading

Encyclopedia Brown, Boy Detective by Donald J. Sobol

How could Sally show more respect to others when she stands up for those who are being bullied?

GUIDING CHILDREN'S LEARNING

1. Begin the lesson by introducing the *Heart Attributes* for the week, ACCEPTANCE and KINDNESS.

2. It's Story Time! Read aloud or listen to the recording of **To Laugh or Not to Laugh?**
   Note: *Guiming* is pronounced "Gway-ming".

3. After the story, explain that this is a *Finish Me Story*. First, have students finish the story. Next, have an open-ended discussion with them, asking what they believe Tommy should do when he sees that Guiming has overheard the comments from his fellow classmates.

   - What do you think of the students' talk about Guiming?
   - How do you think Guiming feels on his first day of school?
   - Should Tommy say something to the other students about their behavior?
   - What should Tommy say to Guiming?
   - Should Tommy say something to Mr. Watson, the teacher?

MANNERS IN ACTION

1. Review the definitions of the *Heart Attributes*, ACCEPTANCE and KINDNESS.

2. Discuss these *Big Ideas* with your children:
   - It is important to stand up for someone who is being bullied.
   - When you see bullying, talk to those who are being unkind.
   - When you see bullying, talk to a responsible adult who can help.

3. How can we demonstrate ACCEPTANCE and KINDNESS? Challenge your students to look for opportunities to show KINDNESS and ACCEPTANCE this week. *There are people all around us who need someone to accept them and to be kind to them. Whether at home or at school, be intentional this week and look for those who may be having a bad day.*

Day 1

TO LAUGH OR NOT TO LAUGH?

Once upon a heart in Merryville, muffled laughter trickled out of the last classroom in the hallway. Tommy stopped humming, so he could listen. Curious, he tiptoed to the door and pushed it just a bit open.

Tommy was late to school that morning because of a doctor's appointment. And today was a big day, so he had been eager to get back. Everyone had been told that a brand new student was starting and that he had moved all the way from China, which was literally on the opposite side of the world. It was strange to Tommy to think that a family would move from a huge, busy place like China to a tiny, quiet town like Merryville.

He had heard the student's name was Guiming. He had trouble saying it and had no idea how to spell it. When he had mentioned this to his parents, they had smiled and explained that a name like Guiming might be just as common in China as the name Tommy was in America.

They told him that China had a language full of completely different sounds and words, words that Tommy wouldn't have ever imagined could exist.

Tommy cracked the door of the classroom wider and peered in. He couldn't see a teacher, just a crowd of students around a desk.

"Did you see Guiming? Wow, I think he missed a little food from his lunch today," one boy was cackling, pointing to his own face sarcastically.

"Yeah, what is it, anyway? A birthmark or some kind of tattoo? It's gross! And right on his face!"

"Hey Guiming, the ketchup goes on your fries, not your face!"

The boys laughed loudly, encouraging each other in their cutting remarks.

Tommy heard something behind him. When he turned to look, he saw someone standing right next to him that he didn't recognize.

This must be Guiming, Tommy thought, realizing all at once that Guiming must have heard every word. The first thing he noticed was that Guiming had a huge birthmark on his left cheek. It looked like a big dark splotch that ran messily from his left nostril almost to his chin. It was hard not to notice it.

Before he could say anything, the kids looked up and saw Tommy and Guiming standing in the doorway. It was easy to see they were worried that a teacher was coming or that they had been overheard.

"Hey, Tommy," Wesley said awkwardly, "meet Guiming."

Guiming turned and extended his hand. "Hey!" Tommy said, shaking his hand.

Then suddenly and nervously, as though they couldn't help it, the group of boys started laughing all over again. Tommy looked over at Wesley who was doubled over and almost crying from laughing so much. Then Tommy stole a glance at Guiming who let out a loud, short laugh, and was turning deep red. He wasn't smiling at all, just forcing a laugh. Tommy knew that laugh—the embarrassed, fake laugh you give when you pretend to make fun of yourself like everybody else.

The bell rang and the rest of the class filed in. Mr. Watson called everyone to order and then introduced Guiming to everyone in class. Before long, the students were diving into fractions and whole numbers. Most of the students were not aware of what had happened right before the bell, but Tommy looked over at Guiming, fully aware that Guiming had not forgotten.

After class, Tommy saw Guiming walk hurriedly over to the far corner of the schoolyard, closest to the shade trees. He was alone. Instinctively, Tommy began to follow him, but hesitated. *Maybe he doesn't want to talk to anyone right now. Then again...*

The pit in Tommy's stomach didn't seem to be going anywhere...

A Finish Me Story: What should Tommy do now?

7 Being A Buddy, Not A Bully

Day 2 MUSIC OF THE HEART®

1. This lesson teaches students what to do when they see someone being bullied.

2. Here are three steps to deter bullying:
   Step 1: *Don't stand back.*
   Step 2: *Step in* for the one being bullied and ask a friend to join you.
   - To the bully, point out the wrong they are doing by saying, "That's not funny," or something similar. When kids step in and defend the one being bullied, they give others who are standing by confidence to speak up.
   - To the one being bullied, tell him/her you are there to help. When kids befriend a child who is being bullied, bullies are less likely to pick on that child. Friendship can also give children support and confidence to stand up for themselves.
   Step 3: *Stand up* and find a teacher, parent, or responsible adult to confront the bully. Sometimes kids who are bullied are scared to ask an adult for help because they think it will make the bullying worse.

3. Teach the **Don't Stand Back** chant with the motions.

You'll Need:
- Don't Stand Back video
- Don't Stand Back activity sheet

Day 3 WRITING FROM THE HEART

Ask your students to consider the following journal prompt and answer it according to your classroom writing requirements:

Can you think of a time you could have stood up for someone who was being bullied, but did not? Is it easy to stand up and step in when someone is being bullied? Why or why not?

You'll Need:
- Being a Buddy, Not a Bully activity sheet (1/student)

Days 2-5

Day 4   CREATIVE CONNECTION

1. Give each student an activity sheet.

2. Lead the following discussion:
   - *What is in the heart of a bully?*
     Anger, hurt, sadness, meanness
   - *What is in the heart of a buddy?*
     Happiness, love, kindness, respect
   - *How can we help those being bullied?*
     Stand up for them and step in to stop the bullying.
     Bullies can be stopped and turned around so they stop hurting others.

3. Have students fill the hearts with words describing the heart of a BULLY and a BUDDY.

4. Share with the class.

You'll Need:
- **Bully & Buddy** activity sheet (1 set/student)
- Pencils

Day 5   TECH TIME

Interactive Whiteboard Activity on MyManners Portal

Meet the meanest girl in second grade!

MANNERS IN ACTION

Whooooo will hang the **Happle** this week?

ACCEPTANCE—Treating everyone you meet with the same respect, regardless of differences

KINDNESS—Showing care for others in an unexpected and exceptional way

WEEK 8
FOLLOWING THE GOLDEN RULE

Big Ideas

- A child who learns to love well learns to live well.
- When you look inside someone's heart, you find they have the same needs you do—to love and be loved.
- A child who experiences the love found in the Golden Rule develops the desire to live by the Golden Rule.

For Your Heart

It would be difficult to find someone who does not know the Golden Rule—Treat others the way you would like to be treated. Despite this, we often see the following:

Those who live by the Silver Rule—"Do not harm anyone if you do not want them to harm you."

Those who live by the Brass Rule—"I'll treat you the way you treat me."

Those who live by the Iron Rule—"What is yours is mine when I take it by force."

The Golden Rule calls us to love our fellow man without reserve. When we live by the Golden Rule and teach our children to do the same, we demonstrate:

- Respecting others the way we would like to be respected.
- Having patience with others the way we would like others to have patience with us.
- Caring for others the way we would like to be cared for.
- Loving others the way we would like to be loved.

The Golden Rule calls us to love our fellow man without reserve.

For the Hearts of Your Students

Today's society doesn't encourage the Golden Rule. Children see adults around them who don't have respect for others, who display a lack of patience and caring of others. You can lead by example by practicing the Golden Rule with your students and peers.

In this week's lesson, you have the privilege of undertaking the mission to help your students develop *empathy* and *humility*, enabling them to put the Golden Rule into action. Developing the ability to walk in another person's shoes is rooted in a deep sense of humility—not caring who gets the credit. It is doing the right thing because it is the right thing to do. You can be the one to show your students what the rest of the world is not showing them—how much better life can be when we focus on taking care of each other's hearts the way we would like for others to take care of our own hearts!

8 Following The Golden Rule

EMPATHY—Walking in another person's shoes

HUMILITY—Not caring who gets credit

REMEMBER

SKILLS AND OBJECTIVES

- Children will learn to look into the hearts of others to see what they need.
- Children will learn to look past the troubles on the outside and see the struggles on the inside.
- Children will learn to treat others in the way their hearts want to be treated.

Wise Ol' Wilbur's Recommended Reading

I am Anne Frank
by Brad Meltzer

Does Anne treat others the way she would like to be treated? How was this especially difficult for her and her family?

GUIDING CHILDREN'S LEARNING

1. Introduce the definitions for this week's *Heart Attributes*: EMPATHY and HUMILITY. Encourage the students to memorize and recite the definitions. They should also listen closely to the story for examples of both *Heart Attributes*.

2. Let's Listen! Read aloud or play the recording of **The Shirt off His Back**.

3. After the story, lead your students in the following discussion questions:
   - *What did Tommy notice about his new friend, Phillip?*
     He noticed that he was wearing the same shirt over and over and that it was worn.
   - *Did Phillip tell Tommy he needed a new shirt? Why not?*
     No. Perhaps he was embarrassed.
   - *What shirts of his own did Tommy pick out for Phillip?*
     Tommy picked out two of his favorite, newer shirts.
   - *What does that tell you?*
     Tommy gave Phillip what he would have wanted to be given to him!
   - *What do you think of the way Tommy got the shirts to Phillip?*
     Tommy protected Phillip's feelings by being careful that no one saw what he was doing, not even Phillip!

MANNERS IN ACTION

1. At the end of the discussion, point out the **Happle Tree** and how the number of **Happles** is growing. Remind your students that their hearts are growing as well!

2. Discuss these *Big Ideas* with your students:
   - We must look into the hearts of others to see their needs.
   - Sometimes people don't ask for help, because they are embarrassed.
   - We find the needs of others when we imagine "walking in their shoes."

3. Ask your students how they can show EMPATHY and HUMILITY this week. Encourage students to look for opportunities to think about the circumstances of others. Is there something they can do to help others without trying to get the credit for it? Sometimes it's possible to help someone else out and they never find out who did it! If it's not possible to keep it a secret, then it is best to keep it quiet and not brag! Go out and treat others the way you want to be treated this week!

Day 1

THE SHIRT OFF HIS BACK

Once upon a heart in Merryville, on the first day of school, Tommy Tripper noticed there was a new kid at Merryville Elementary. Since Tommy was the new kid last year, he decided he would make friends with the new boy because he had wanted a friend when he first came to Merryville.

When recess came, Tommy walked over to the new kid who was sitting in the gravel. He sat down next to him and said, "Hi, my name is Tommy, Tommy Tripper. What's yours?"

"Hey," said the new kid, picking up some gravel and letting it fall through his fingers. "My name is Phillip."

"It's nice to meet you, Phillip. I was the new kid last year. I remember how scared I was the first day of school," answered Tommy. "Do you want to sit with my friends and me at lunch?"

Phillip looked up with lonely eyes at Tommy and nodded his head yes.

A week went by, and Tommy became one of Phillip's close friends. Every other day after school, they went to the park and played fetch with Buddy, Bully, and PD the puppy dog. On the other days, they rode their bikes all over Merryville. On the weekends, they had fun at the beach looking for seashells. Sometimes, they joined Mrs. McDonald and Cap'n Nick on long walks along the seashore.

After a couple more weeks, Tommy noticed that Phillip wore the same navy and grey striped shirt with a hole in the side every day. Each day that Tommy saw the shirt, he wondered if that was the only shirt Philip had. He didn't want to ask because he didn't want to make Philip feel bad.

When Tommy got home, he ran to his room and dug through his drawers like PD does when he digs up a bone. Tommy grabbed two of his favorite shirts and went to the kitchen to get a paper bag. He stuffed the shirts into the bag and put the bag into his backpack to take to school the next day.

Tommy was so excited that he could hardly sleep. When his mom called him for breakfast the next morning, he ate faster than he had ever eaten before. He couldn't wait to get to school, but before he walked out the door, he told his mom what he wanted to do for Phillip and asked her advice on how to give Phillip the shirts without embarrassing him. After brainstorming a few ideas, they decided Tommy would wait until lunch time and put the paper bag into Phillip's backpack.

When he rode down to school, Tommy saw Phillip and Wesley and joined them. The three boys headed in the school together and down the hall to Mrs. Sweetwater's classroom.

Throughout the day, Tommy watched for a chance to put the shirts in Phillip's backpack when no one else would see him. When everyone went to lunch, Tommy stayed behind and slipped the paper bag into Phillip's backpack. He joined his friends in the cafeteria without saying a word. After lunch, they went to Mr. Smith's class.

"Class, get out your math books," Mr. Smith said, as he picked up his own textbook. Everyone in the class began to dig through their backpacks for their math books. Tommy grabbed his book quickly and looked up just as Philip opened his backpack. Philip reached in and then found the paper bag. His eyes grew wide when he opened the bag and saw the two shirts. He looked around the room to see if anyone was watching. He hung his head sadly at first, but then smiled when he realized someone had done something so kind.

Phillip didn't see Tommy was watching. Tommy smiled too, because this was the first time he had ever seen Phillip really smile.

Helping is a good thing, even if no one asks, Tommy thought, as he opened his math book to the page Mr. Smith had given him.

Just the beginning...

8 Following The Golden Rule

Day 2 ART OF THE HEART®

1. Tell your children we're going to take a look into our hearts and see what's there!

2. Give each child a copy of **Wilbur's Glasses** activity sheet. Ask them to cut out the glasses and then glue an arm to each side of the glasses.

3. Set the glasses aside for Day 4!

You'll Need:
- **Wilbur's Glasses** activity sheet (1/student, preferably printed on cardstock)
- Scissors
- Glue

Day 3 WRITING FROM THE HEART

Ask your students to consider the following journal prompt and answer it according to your classroom writing requirements:

Treating others the way I want to be treated means...

You'll Need:
- **Following the Golden Rule** activity sheet (1/student)

Days 2-5

Day 4 CREATIVE CONNECTION

1. Ask students to take out their **Wilbur Glasses** from Day 2.

2. Hand out the **What's on the Inside Shows on the Outside** activity sheets. Ask your students to put their glasses on and look at the sheet.

3. Go through the activity by asking your students the following questions while they circle the correct answers:
   - *If you have love in your heart, will you hit someone or hug someone?*
   - *If you have patience in your heart, will you wait or will you whine?*
   - *If you have kindness in your heart, will you help someone or hurt someone?*
   - *If you have sadness in your heart, will you cry or will you laugh?*
   - *If you have anger in your heart, will you hug or will you hit?*
   - *If you have self-control in your heart, will you talk or will you listen when someone else is talking?*
   - *If you have joy in your heart, will you smile or will you frown?*
   - *If you have selfishness in your heart, will you take or will you give?*

You'll Need:
- **Wilbur's Glasses** from Day 2
- **What's on the Inside Shows on the Outside** activity sheet (1/student)
- Pencils

Day 5 TECH TIME

Interactive Whiteboard Activity on MyManners Portal

Let's go Happle picking this week!

MANNERS IN ACTION

Whooooo will hang the **Happle** this week?

EMPATHY—Walking in another person's shoes
HUMILITY—Not caring who gets credit

WEEK 9
BECOMING LADIES AND GENTLEMEN

Big Ideas

- A girl who respects others becomes a lady who respects herself.
- A boy with a kind heart becomes a man with a good heart.
- Habits children develop in childhood help shape who they become as adults and therefore, who we become as a society.

For Your Heart

Many of us were expected to say "Yes, Ma'am" and "Yes, Sir" as children to show respect for authority. We were taught to never, under any circumstance, say an unkind word about anyone.

Saying "Have a good day!" when parting someone's company felt as natural as saying "Hello!" Stepping aside and opening doors for adults happened without forethought when you had been encouraged to show respect for others as long as you could remember.

Teaching common courtesies was once considered essential to a child's upbringing and helped maintain a certain level of order and civility in our society. Without these common courtesies, we have seen a rise in incivility in all aspects of our culture.

To reclaim the same level of civility we once enjoyed, we must begin to teach our children these basic courtesies.

For the Hearts of Your Students

Well-developed manners in young children become the foundation for morals in the teenage years and beyond. You have the privilege of helping your girls discover how special it is to become a lady. Teach your girls to encourage boys to treat them as ladies should be treated, and you will support the development of self-respect in their own hearts.

When you teach young boys how to treat girls with respect, they restrain from inappropriate behavior as they grow up. In becoming gentlemen, your boys will begin to put the needs of others ahead of their own.

In this week's lesson, each grade level will focus on a different aspect of helping students become *gentle* and *gracious* as they develop good manners over the course of early childhood.

9 Becoming Ladies and Gentlemen

GENTLE—Speaking and acting with tenderness

GRACIOUS—Being polite, understanding and generous in all situations

REMEMBER

SKILLS AND OBJECTIVES

- Children will learn to be ladies and gentlemen by showing respect to others.
- Girls will learn to allow a boy to treat them like a lady.
- Boys will learn various ways to act like a gentleman by putting ladies first.

Confessions of a Former Bully by Trudy Ludwig

How did Katie learn to stop bullying?

GUIDING CHILDREN'S LEARNING

1. Introduce the definitions for this week's *Heart Attributes*: GRACIOUS and GRACIOUS. Encourage the students to memorize and recite the definitions. They should also listen closely to the story for examples of both *Heart Attributes*.

2. Let's Listen! Read aloud or play the recording of **Rescue at the Fall Fair** 🖥️❤️

3. After the story, lead your students in the following discussion questions:
   - *Brianna got onstage to sing the Star-Spangled Banner, but what happened?*
     She began singing the wrong song, and some people laughed and she felt embarrassed.
   - *What did Mary do? How did this show GRACIOUSNESS and GENTLENESS for Brianna?*
     Mary began singing the song along with her, even though it wasn't the right song. By joining Brianna in singing, she encouraged her and showed her she wasn't alone. Mary did this because she cared about Brianna's feelings.
   - *How did Brianna feel when Mary and the others sang with her?*
     She felt the others cared for her and didn't want her to be embarrassed.
   - *Explain how Mary's and the other students' actions showed GENTLE and GRACIOUS hearts.* (Answers will vary)
   - *Have you ever felt that your friends or family "rescued" you from feeling embarrassed?* (Answers will vary)

MANNERS IN ACTION

1. At the end of the discussion, point out the **Happle Tree** and how the number of **Happles** is growing. Remind your students that their hearts are growing as well!

2. Discuss these *Big Ideas* with your students:
   - Being a lady or a gentleman means that you are GENTLE.
   - Being a lady or gentleman means that you are GRACIOUS and careful with the feelings of others.
   - Respect is an important part of becoming a lady or a gentleman.

3. Encourage your students that being a lady or a gentleman will earn them respect from others. When they conduct themselves with GRACE and GENTLENESS, people will be drawn to them and respect them. What particular things can they do this week to show that they are growing into young ladies and gentlemen?

Day 1

RESCUE AT THE FALL FAIR

Once upon a heart in Merryville, the long, cool days of October told everyone the time for the annual Fall Fair at Merryville Elementary had arrived. Mothers and dads, grandparents, aunts and uncles all came to the school for good old-fashioned fun.

Each year, a different class is given the honor of serving as hosts and hostesses of the fair. They have three main duties: to greet everyone as they enter the fairgrounds, to give directions to the games and to hand out programs for the special show at the end of the day.

Everyone was really excited because they get to carry on a tradition that has lasted many, many years in Merryville—the singing of "The Star Spangled Banner" to close the show. The children worked for weeks and weeks perfecting the song. They practiced their lines and memorized the words.

The big day finally came. Everyone was having a good time. Wesley won the watermelon-eating contest for the second year in a row. Trey won the softball throw when his ball was the only ball to go through a tiny hoop. The dunking booth had the longest line, because everyone wanted to see Mr. Stiglets, the school principal, land in the water and come up laughing.

Right in the middle of all the fun, the schoolyard bell rang, signaling the big show was about to begin. Mr. Stiglets got out of his wet clothes. Miss Charlotte covered her table of chocolate goodies with a cloth to protect them from Carolina, Mrs. McDonald's yard cow who loves milk chocolate.

The children ran backstage in the auditorium to get ready for the show while the adults found their seats. Brianna and Jasmine huddled together with Mary, Allie and Caroline to go through the words of the closing song one more time.

When all the children were ready, Miss Carter, the music director, led them outside the auditorium to line up at the front door.

Mr. Stiglets welcomed everyone. The drums rolled and the cymbals clashed as the doors opened for the kids to march down the aisles to the stage. Everyone in the room jumped to their feet and cheered. The show had begun!

The kindergartners took turns acting out their favorite nursery rhymes. The first graders shared artwork and poems they had written. Each of the third graders played a different musical instrument, including a xylophone, a triangle, a wooden block, a harmonica, hand bells and even a keyboard. It was a great show!

When the time came for the grand finale, the kids lined up with their black top hats and red bowties. Brianna stepped forward to sing the first line of "The Star Spangled Banner" all by herself.

Miss Carter played a note on the piano to set the pitch for Brianna. Brianna took a deep breath and started singing, "O beautiful for spacious skies…"

That was the opening line, but it was the wrong song. A few people gasped as everyone realized she was singing the wrong words. A few people even started laughing. Brianna didn't know what to do. She was so embarrassed, she just stopped. Tears ran down her face.

Just as she turned to run off the stage, Mary stopped her and picked up right where she left off, "…for amber ways of grain."

Jasmine and Allie chimed in.

"For purple mountains majesty, above the fruited plains."

Terrell, Trey, Wesley and Tommy joined Caroline as she raised her hands for everyone in the audience to join in, "America, America, God shed his grace on thee."

The laughter stopped and everyone began singing. When it was done, Brianna hugged her friends and thanked them for rescuing her. They all turned to the flag and placed their hands over their hearts. This time when Miss Carter gave the pitch, together they sang, "O, say can you see by the dawn's early light…"

As the students carefully sang each heartfelt line of the song, the audience began to join in. One by one, they stood and placed their own hands on their hearts until together, they belted out the last line: "O'er the land of the free and the home of the brave."

Another grand ending to a great Merryville Fall Fair!

Just the beginning…

9 Becoming Ladies and Gentlemen

Day 2 MUSIC OF THE HEART®

1. Give each boy and girl an activity sheet. Explain that they will read through these **Codes of Honor** and then sign them when they are ready.

2. Teach students that both ladies and gentlemen care for the feelings of others by acting and speaking respectfully. Remind them that practicing now helps them as they grow older. Both ladies and gentlemen show respect by:
   - Never saying mean things about someone else
   - Saying "Sir" and "Ma'am" to adults
   - Giving their seats to adults
   - Holding doors open for adults
   - Saying "Please", "Thank you", and "Excuse me"
   - Never using curse words

3. Boys show they are gentlemen by paying attention to the needs of those around them and doing what they can to meet these needs. Examples:
   - Opening doors for ladies/adults and allowing them to enter/exit first
   - Pulling out a lady's chair at the table to help her sit down
   - Offering to help a girl carry heavy things
   - Removing their hats indoors, especially in the presence of ladies

4. Girls show they are ladies by accepting the kindness of a gentleman and also paying attention to the needs of those around them and doing what they can to help the person in need.

You'll Need:
- Soft music played in the background
- **My Code of Honor** activity sheets (1/boys, 1/girls)

Day 3 WRITING FROM THE HEART

Ask your students to consider the following journal prompt and answer it according to your classroom writing requirements:

Do you think acting like ladies and gentlemen is just for adults? Why would it be good to learn these manners as a third grader?

You'll Need:
- **Becoming Ladies and Gentlemen** activity sheet (1/student)

Days 2-5

Day 4 CREATIVE CONNECTION

1. Ask your students to look at the activity sheets. Remind them of what they learned on Day 2.

2. Do a role-play for your students to practice these new skills.
   - Ladies, please get up from your seats with a book in your hand. (Boys should rise and offer to carry their books. Girls accept help graciously.)
   - Ladies, please walk to the door (Boys should walk to the door to open it. Girls thank boys for their help.)
   - Ladies, please return to your seats (Boys follow and pull out chairs.)
   - Ladies, please take a seat (Boys should help push in their chair and sit after girls are seated. Girls thank boys for their kindness.)

3. Close the lesson with the following points:
   - Sometimes it is hard to be kind and notice the needs of others, and it can be even harder to politely accept kindness from others.
   - It is important to start practicing ways to be a lady and a gentleman today to show your maturity. Practicing today will help you form good habits when you are older.

You'll Need:
- Soft music playing in the background
- **My Code of Honor** activity sheets

Day 5 TECH TIME

Interactive Whiteboard Activity on MyManners Portal

Unscramble the code to find out more about honor!

MANNERS IN ACTION

Whooooo will hang the **Happle** this week?

GENTLE—Speaking and acting with tenderness
GRACIOUS—Being polite, understanding and generous in all situations

WEEK 10
BEING A HOST

Big Ideas

- Being a good host shows your guest how much you care.
- Good hosts are generous with their belongings.
- Hospitable hosts make their guests feel loved.

For Your Heart

Webster defines host as "one granting hospitality, one in charge of guests." If you combine these definitions, the best understanding of host becomes "guest master", a meaningful old term rarely used today.

You don't need a big house with fancy things to be a "guest master". You only need a heart to serve others and a desire to make others feel better than they did before they came to see you. Author and educator, Henrietta Mears, once said, "Hospitality should have no other nature than love." In other words, a hospitable host makes his or her guest feel loved.

Helping your students become "guest masters" begins with modeling hospitality as you greet and dismiss them. Take a few minutes every day to show your students that they are welcomed and loved. Stand at the door and greet each child by name with a smile and a handshake or a hug. Call them by name and let them see how special each one is to you. When they leave, do the same. They will see your classroom as a safe and loving place and look forward to coming every day!

For the Hearts of Your Students

Students consistently rate this lesson as *the* favorite because it makes them feel important. They rise to the occasion when asked to open the classroom door and greet a visitor. They love walking a guest to the door and saying, "Thank you for visiting our class."

In this week's lesson, you'll encourage your students to take on the role of being responsible hosts who take care of others. You'll help them experience the joy that comes from showing *hospitality* through acts of *generosity*.

You can take pleasure in watching your students develop generous hearts focused on meeting the needs of others. Giving your students opportunities to practice being hosts will enable them to give love and receive love.

10 Being a Host

HOSPITALITY—Serving others so they feel cared for and comfortable

GENEROSITY—Gladly giving my time, talent and treasure

REMEMBER

SKILLS AND OBJECTIVES

- Children will learn how to be a good host.
- Children will learn how to plan a party.
- Children will learn to look for ways for guests to feel welcome.

Wise Ol' Wilbur's Recommended Reading

The Littles
by John Peterson

Would you want to visit the Littles? Why or why not?

GUIDING CHILDREN'S LEARNING

1. Introduce the definitions for this week's *Heart Attributes*: HOSPITALITY and GENEROSITY. Encourage the students to memorize and recite the definitions. They should also listen closely to the story for examples of both *Heart Attributes*.

2. Let's Listen! Read aloud or play the recording of ***Allie's Party***

3. After the story, lead your students in the following discussion questions:
   - *Why were friends going over to Allie's house?*
     It was her birthday!
   - *Did it seem that Allie and her mom were prepared for their guests?*
     Yes! They had made cookies, planned a spaghetti dinner, movie and games.
   - *Overall, how would you describe Caroline's behavior?*
     She was picky, ungrateful and complaining.
   - *How did Allie react to Caroline?*
     She continued to be kind and patient.
   - *What gift seemed to turn Caroline's heart around?*
     The friendship bracelet.
   - *Describe Caroline's behavior at the end of the story.*
     She was apologetic and asked Allie and her mom to forgive her. She finally began to enjoy herself.

MANNERS IN ACTION

1. At the end of the discussion, point out the **Happle Tree** and how the number of **Happles** is growing. Remind your students that their hearts are growing as well!

2. Discuss these *Big Ideas* with your students:
   - *When we invite someone to be our guest, it is our job to help them feel welcome.*
   - *Offering a guest refreshments and asking them what they would like to do is part of being a good host.*
   - *Planning a party is a lot of work, but it is fun!*

3. Ask your children how they can show HOSPITALITY and GENEROSITY this week. Learning to plan a time with others as our guests is a valuable skill. There are many opportunities for us to make certain those around us have what they need. Sometimes, they only need to be introduced to others so they feel comfortable. Challenge the students to practice being HOSPITABLE and GENEROUS this week.

Day 1

ALLIE'S PARTY

Once upon a heart in Merryville, eager students waited for the last bell of the day on a Friday afternoon. Allie and her friends were especially excited. It was her birthday, and three of her friends were coming home with her for a sleepover! When the bell rang, the girls quickly gathered their things and headed to Allie's house.

Soon, the girls were greeted by Allie's mother with hugs and sugar cookies. The other girls gobbled up their cookies, but Allie's friend, Caroline, frowned and began to complain. "I don't really like sugar cookies. Don't you have chocolate chip instead?" Surprised, Allie's mother said, "I'm sorry, Caroline, but this is all we have."

After the snack, the girls went out to play. But after only a few minutes, Caroline groaned, "It's too hot out here! Let's go inside and play games."

Allie and the other girls didn't really want to go inside yet, but Allie said, "Come on. Let's go inside with Caroline." She did not want Caroline to be alone, so they all went inside and played some board games.

When it was time for dinner, Allie's mom called the girls to the table. Allie cheered when she saw her favorite dinner—spaghetti! But Caroline sighed and looked down at her plate. "Allie," she whined, "I thought you said we were having pizza!"

Allie's mom smiled and said, "Since it's Allie's birthday, I decided to make her favorite supper as a surprise, but we do have a small frozen pizza. Would you like for me to put that in the oven for you?"

Caroline nodded with relief and didn't seem to mind that Allie's mother had to begin baking a pizza after working so hard to have a delicious spaghetti dinner ready for everyone else.

After dinner, the girls sat down to watch a movie before bed. It didn't surprise anyone when Caroline said, "I saw this movie last week! I don't want to watch it again." Allie's mom told Caroline that Allie had picked the movie because she thought Caroline would enjoy it. Caroline didn't seem to care and couldn't stand seeing the other girls having fun. Not long after, Caroline just rolled over in her sleeping bag and went to sleep mad.

The girls decided to enjoy the movie and let Caroline sleep. As Allie crawled into her own sleeping bag, she felt disappointed and a little sad that Caroline did not seem to be enjoying herself. She decided to give Caroline an extra hug in the morning, then she closed her eyes and fell fast asleep.

The next morning, Allie and her friends woke to the smell of sausage and pancakes. Allie wanted to help her mom, but decided it was a good time to give her friend a special surprise. "Caroline, I have something for you." She brought Caroline to her room and handed her a friendship bracelet that she had made all by herself.

Without thinking of her friend's feelings, Caroline took one look at the bracelet and threw it down on the floor. "Eww. I don't like those colors! Don't you have another one?"

Allie turned sadly away, trying to brush away her tears. She left quickly to help her mom with breakfast, while Caroline and the others rolled up their sleeping bags and packed their things.

While she was packing, Caroline picked up her pillow and underneath, found Allie's friendship bracelet. In that moment, her heart turned from mad to sad. She thought about what a good host Allie was trying to be. "Maybe it's not her fault I've been unhappy. Maybe it's my fault."

Slipping on the bracelet, Caroline went quietly to the kitchen, enjoyed the delicious breakfast, and thanked Allie's mom. "Mrs. Roberts," Caroline said quietly, "I'm sorry I was so ugly last night. The others girls said your sugar cookies were the best and I can't believe you gave me pizza instead of spaghetti. Can you ever forgive me?"

Mrs. Roberts put her arm around Caroline and answered, "Sometimes we all forget our manners. You are very brave to come and talk to me." After breakfast, the girls ran outside and played together for the rest of the morning.

When it was time for everyone to leave, Caroline hugged Allie and whispered, "Allie? I'm so sorry I was mean to you. You were nice to me the whole time I was here, even though I never stopped complaining." Allie saw the friendship bracelet on Caroline's wrist and gave her friend a hug.

"I forgive you, Caroline. You're my good friend, and you are my guest, too," said Allie.

"Thank you, Allie! And Happy, Happy Birthday! This was the best slumber party I've ever been to," said Caroline. "I'm so happy to have you as my friend!"

Just the beginning...

10 Being a Host

Day 2 ART OF THE HEART®

1. Discuss:
   - *What does it mean to be a "host"?*
     To have a friend or relative over
     To play with a friend at your house
   - *What does it mean to be a "guest"?*
     To visit someone else's home
   - *Has anyone heard the word hospitality before?*
     The word HOSPITALITY has to do with being a good host.

2. Pass out the activity sheets.

3. Explain that this activity sheet outlines some of the most important manners of a good host.

4. Have the students unscramble the letters and color in the balloons.

5. Read the sentences aloud and discuss.

You'll Need:
- **Being a Host Word Scramble** activity sheet
- Pencils
- Crayons

Day 3 WRITING FROM THE HEART

1. Give each student a **Party Planning** activity sheet and have them work in groups or individually.
2. Tell your students they are going to IMAGINE the greatest party ever and celebrate someone who is very special to them! Have them share their creative ideas with the class!

You'll Need:
- **Party Planning** activity sheet
- Pencil

Days 2-5

Day 4 CREATIVE CONNECTION

1. Have your students pull out their **Party Planning** activity sheets from Day 3 and pass out the **You're Invited!** activity sheets.

2. Follow the instructions to create pretend invitations to the parties they planned very carefully on Day 3.

3. Have your students share their ideas for what they have imagined to be the greatest party ever!

4. Ask them why they chose their guest of honor and how they believe that person would feel if they were really able to throw a party for them.

You'll Need:
- **You're Invited!** activity sheet
- **Party Planning** activity sheets from Day 3
- Colored pencils

Day 5 TECH TIME

Interactive Whiteboard Activity on MyManners Portal

Choose a cupcake to test your guest etiquette!

MANNERS IN ACTION

Whoooooo will hang the **Happle** this week?

HOSPITALITY—Serving others so they feel cared for and comfortable
GENEROSITY—Gladly giving my time, talent and treasure

WEEK 11
BEING A GUEST

Big Ideas

- Appreciating the hospitality of your host is the beginning of being a good guest.

- Acknowledging value in people, places and things is at the heart of being a good guest.

- Polite behavior shows the appreciation in your heart for the privilege of visiting in someone's home, office or school.

For Your Heart

When my twin sons were seven years old, we attempted to have a classmate over after a soccer game one Saturday. Mike (name changed to protect the guilty) complained that fishing in the nearby pond was "boring," the picnic lunch was "stupid," and making homemade chocolate chip cookies was "for girls." These activities were top-of-the-list by other friends who came to visit, but not Mike. He was miserable and made us miserable, too.

The boys could invite other friends over to enjoy all of these activities, but Mike didn't receive many invitations because he was such a complainer. He wasn't willing to try new things or show appreciation for the opportunity to be with friends.

We all know it wasn't Mike's fault. No one taught him how to appreciate being a guest in someone's home. No one taught him to be polite to a host who welcomed him in. He was accustomed to getting things his way or no way. So, he found himself with no way to have fun.

For the Hearts of Your Students

Just as you had the opportunity to show your students how to be good hosts, you can help them learn to be good guests. How grateful your students will be to learn the pleasure of getting along by going along. Just imagine their delight when they're invited back to a friend's house for a return visit because they've become a favorite guest.

In this week's lesson, you'll help your students learn how to be *grateful* for their host's hospitality by offering *polite* gestures through words and actions. This is a practical lesson that instills valuable social skills that will take them into places beyond their wildest imaginings as welcomed guests one day. Equipping your students to be good guests is one of the most important lessons you can impart to ensure their success in life and living.

11 Being a Guest

GRATEFUL—Giving thanks from the heart

POLITE—Using kind words and actions in all situations

REMEMBER

SKILLS AND OBJECTIVES

- Children will learn polite words and actions as a guest.
- Children will learn to participate in party games and activities.
- Children will learn the importance of a thank you note.

Stuart Little
by E.B. White

What evidence can you find that Stuart is polite?

GUIDING CHILDREN'S LEARNING

1. Begin the lesson by introducing this week's *Heart Attributes*: GRATEFUL and POLITE. Review the definitions throughout the week.

2. Let's Listen! Read aloud or play the recording of ***The Big, Little Guest***

3. After the story, lead your students in the following discussion questions:
   - *How are Alston and Wesley related to one another?*
     Alston is Wesley's younger cousin.
   - *How would you describe Alston?*
     He is physically small and nervous about going to a party where he doesn't know very many people. He is fast!
   - *What things did Alston do to try to fit in?*
     He offered to get Terrell something to drink and jumped right in to play dodgeball.
   - *How did Wesley help to turn things around so the other guests would include Alston?*
     After the game, he realized that Alston was not being accepted by his friends. He invited Alston to stand next to him and hand him the gifts.
   - *What happened when everyone saw Wesley making room for Alston?*
     They accepted him as well.

MANNERS IN ACTION

1. At the end of the discussion, point out the **Happle Tree** and how the number of **Happles** is growing. Remind your students that their hearts are growing as well!

2. Discuss these *Big Ideas* with your students:
   - *We should always show GRATITUDE for being someone's guest.*
   - *Sometimes it's uncomfortable to be a guest when you don't know many people.*
   - *Always use POLITE words and actions as someone's guest.*

3. Ask your children to share times they have been invited to be someone's guest. What POLITE words and actions should we demonstrate to show that we are GRATEFUL for the invitation? Be on the lookout this week for the students who are showing others that they are GRATEFUL and POLITE. These students will hang the Happles on the Happle Tree!

Day 1

THE BIG, LITTLE GUEST

Once upon a heart in Merryville, Alston and his family arrived in town for Wesley's big birthday party. Even though Alston and Wesley were cousins, they didn't see each other often. And Alston was younger, so when Wesley's friends came around, Alston usually stayed quiet. He was hoping he could get to know Wesley's friends better at the birthday party.

Wesley's best friend, Terrell, and his parents, Mr. and Mrs. Brown, hosted the party at the neighborhood park.

"Wesley, I hope I can get to know your friends today," Alston said as he and Wesley rode to the park.

"Well," Wesley replied, "My friends won't ignore you, if you'll just speak up once in a while."

"I can do that," Alston said, hoping he could think of things to say. He was feeling nervous about the whole thing.

Wesley and Alston arrived at the park a few minutes early. Alston shook Mr. Brown's hand and told him he was glad to be invited.

It wasn't long before Wesley's friends got there. Alston was trying hard to think of things to say.

"Hey Terrell," Alston said to Wesley's best friend who was looking for something to drink. "I'll get you something. What would you like?"

"Oh, that's alright I can get it myself," Terrell answered as he pushed passed Alston to find his buddies. This made Alston feel really small. He tried to not let Terrell's attitude bother him, but it sure didn't help his confidence. He looked around the room, swallowed hard, and decided to try again, just as Mrs. Brown called the kids together to play a game.

Mr. Brown tried to divide the kids into two groups for dodge ball, but some of the kids didn't want to play. Alston stepped up, hoping other kids would, too. When the big guys saw Alston standing on the line, they went to the other side, because they didn't want a little guy on their team.

Once the game started, it didn't take long for everyone to see the little guy was faster than all the big guys. He could dodge any ball thrown at him, because he was so quick. He had a can-do attitude that made most people like him, but not Wesley's friends. They just couldn't stand being shown up by a younger kid.

When the game was over, it was time to bring out the birthday cake.

"Happy Birthday to you. Happy birthday to you. Happy birthday, dear Wesley. Happy birthday to you!" the kids sang before Wesley blew out his candles.

Everyone was having a good time. Everyone, that is, but Alston. He had tried so hard to be a good guest and fit in, but Wesley's friends just wouldn't accept him.

Alston didn't know it, but Wesley had seen how his friends mistreated him.

When Wesley started opening his presents, he bypassed all his friends and asked Alston to be the one to sit next to him and hand him the packages.

"Thanks, Wesley," said Alston. "Can Terrell help, too?"

Wesley was surprised by Alston's request, but thought it was mighty big of his little cousin. Wesley's friends thought so, too.

Just the beginning...

11 Being a Guest

Day 2 ART OF THE HEART®

1. Explain that you will be discussing what it means to be a good guest.
2. Pass out the activity sheets and allow the students to color while you discuss the manners of a good guest.
3. Discuss these ideas:
   - *Before you go over:*
     Always ask permission first.
     Ask what you need to bring with you.
     Don't tell others about the invitation, because they may not have been invited.
     Bring a small gift if it is a birthday party.
   - *What should you do while you're there?*
     Follow the rules of the house.
     Say hello to the family members of your host
     Clean up after yourself!
     Respect the belongings in the house.
     Wait for a snack or meal to be offered and served (don't just help yourself!)
     If you do not like something that is served, eat a courtesy bite to show respect for the cook.
     Use polite words.
   - *What should you do when you are leaving?*
     Always say, "Thank you for having me!"
     Always say, "Goodbye."

You'll Need:
- **A Good Guest Says** activity sheet
- Crayons or colored pencils

Day 3 WRITING FROM THE HEART

Ask your students to consider the following journal prompt and answer it according to your classroom writing requirements:

Think about these words:
Hello, Please, Thank you, and Goodbye. Which do you think is the most important? Why? (Hint: there is not a right or wrong answer!)

You'll Need:
- **Being a Guest** activity sheet (1/student)

Days 2-5

Day 4 CREATIVE CONNECTION

1. Give each student a **Thank You Card** activity sheet.
2. Ask them to think of the last time someone had them over as a guest.
3. Ask them to cut out the **Thank You Card** and to take a few minutes to write a note thanking them for their hospitality and kindness.
4. Remind students how special it is to receive a thank you card when you have had someone as your guest.
5. Have your students decorate the card with a special drawing or illustration.
6. Send the cards home with your students and encourage them to deliver them in person or through the mail.

You'll Need:
- **Thank You Card** activity sheet
- Scissors
- Crayons or colored pencils

Day 5 TECH TIME

Interactive Whiteboard Activity on MyManners Portal

Learn how thank you notes can be an enjoyable experience for the writer and the receiever!

MANNERS IN ACTION

Whooooo will hang the **Happle** this week?

GRATEFUL—Giving thanks from the heart
POLITE—Using kind words and actions in all situations

WEEK 12
GREETINGS AND INTRODUCTIONS

Big Ideas

- A heart-felt greeting builds a bridge to others; the absence of a friendly greeting builds a wall.

- A smile breaks through almost any language or cultural barrier. When you smile, the world smiles with you.

- Learning how to greet and introduce others helps young children overcome shyness and uneasiness in social settings.

For Your Heart

In a recent Common Sense Media research study, the average American teenager admitted to preferring texting over talking to other people in person, even friends and family. More than 55% acknowledged that social media keeps them from looking up and talking to people right in front of them.

Haven't you found it more difficult to strike up a conversation in public? It's hard to greet someone on the street, in a store, or at work when no one is looking up. Our screens keep us from acknowledging- perhaps even seeing- one another.

Even at home, we rush through the kitchen without saying, "Good morning" to our family members. We're lost in our screens. Ironically, in this age of digital connection, our society is becoming more disconnected and people are feeling more isolated. Because of this, learning greetings and introductions is more important than ever!

For the Hearts of Your Students

What about your students? Do they greet the bus driver? Do they speak to adults they encounter during the school day? Do they greet you when they enter your classroom? Do they say goodbye when they're leaving?

Let's change the direction society is taking and teach our students to show respect by acknowledging others in the classroom, on the playground, in the halls and cafeteria. When we do this, they will carry the message outside the school building to their homes and communities.

In this week's lesson, you can help your students cultivate *friendliness* by greeting others with openness—a sure sign of *maturity*.

12 Greetings and Introductions

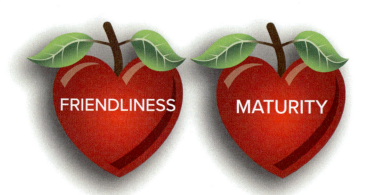

FRIENDLINESS—Welcoming others by offering a quick smile and a kind word

MATURITY—The ability to make the right choice in spite of negative influences

REMEMBER

SKILLS AND OBJECTIVES

- Children will learn to make a good first impression by being polite.
- Children will learn to initiate greetings by shaking hands.
- Children will learn to introduce people in their proper order.

A Bear Called Paddington by Michael Bond

List three things Paddington does that show he is a friendly bear.

GUIDING CHILDREN'S LEARNING

1. Begin the lesson by introducing the *Heart Attributes* for the week, FRIENDLINESS and MATURITY.
2. It's Story Time! Read aloud or listen to the recording of **The Same Drumbeat**
3. After the story, lead your students in the following discussion:
   - *Who is Miguel Rivera?*
     He is a new kid who has just moved to the United States.
   - *Why did Tommy feel that it was difficult to become friends with Miguel?*
     Miguel was more comfortable with his old friends and Miguel had an accent that was hard for Tommy to understand.
   - *How did Tommy include Miguel?*
     He asked him to come on the hike with all his friends.
   - *How do you think Miguel felt around everyone?*
     He was probably a little uncomfortable and lonely.
   - *What did Miguel and Theo have in common?*
     They were both good drummers and they liked the same band.
   - *What had Tommy forgotten to do? How could it have made a difference?*
     He had forgotten to introduce Miguel to all of his friends. If he had introduced them earlier, Theo and Miguel may have talked and found out sooner that they both liked music.

MANNERS IN ACTION

1. Review the definitions of the *Heart Attributes*, FRIENDLINESS and MATURITY.
2. Discuss the following *Big Ideas*:
   - *A first impression is what people first think of you when they meet you.*
   - *It is important to make a good first impression.*
   - *Introducing people who don't know one another helps them feel more comfortable and gives them a good first impression of us.*
3. *How can we demonstrate FRIENDLINESS and MATURITY? Look for those around you who may not be feeling comfortable. Perhaps you could introduce them to some of your friends. When we are FRIENDLY with others, it is a sign of MATURITY. Think about situations that you are in at home or at school where you can reach out to others to help them feel more comfortable.*

Day 1

THE SAME DRUMBEAT

Once upon a heart in Merryville, the whole town was abuzz with news that a new family had moved in from far away. Merryville was a little town and a little out of the way, so it was thrilling to get new arrivals.

Tommy felt special, because his family had gotten to help the Riveras move into their new home. Their son, Miguel, was in Tommy's grade, which was especially exciting. Miguel seemed fun enough. Sometimes though, his accent was difficult for Tommy to understand, and often Miguel got quiet and would withdraw to a corner to stare out the window. Tommy felt sad for him. Surely being in a brand new country, far from the home you loved, was really hard. Realizing Miguel could probably use a distraction, Tommy invited him to hike Merryville Mountain that weekend.

Miguel quickly agreed, and on the day of the hike, was ready with a backpack of snacks and a shy grin. Tommy motioned for him to join the small group of friends as they walked up the lane toward the mountain footpath.

The cliff of Merryville Mountain was one of Tommy's favorite places. It cropped out jaggedly from a smooth, deep slope and every afternoon, without fail, massive gray clouds and flashing thunderstorms amassed in the valley to give every rock climber a spectacular light show.

Tommy noticed that Miguel didn't speak up, except for a shy wave and a "hi." The other kids made Tommy laugh until his sides hurt with all of their inside jokes. Talking with them was so easy, but talking with Miguel felt like work. Tommy had to strain to listen, because Miguel spoke so quietly. And when he spoke about his home country, Tommy could feel his sadness in all the words, even if the word "sad" was never mentioned. Tommy didn't like the way it made him feel, so he usually tried to change the subject.

As they all sat on the cliff to watch and rest, Miguel chose to sit right next to Tommy. Tommy was a little annoyed. Now some of his other friends would have a harder time talking to him. He especially didn't feel like having to do the hard work of listening to every single syllable Miguel tried to say. He simply nodded and then Miguel would nod back.

After a little silence, Miguel pointed to Tommy's shirt, "You like this band too?"

Tommy glanced down at his shirt and realized what he was wearing. "Oh yeah. Yeah I don't mind them."

The conversation fell silent again. It was a little awkward. Tommy wracked his brain for something to say, but he couldn't think of anything. He glanced out of the corner of his eye at Miguel and noticed him shooting quick glances to the other kids.

Suddenly, it occurred to him. He doesn't even know their names. That would be kind of scary: to be surrounded by people you don't know.

Quietly, he heard Miguel begin to tap out the drumbeat of a song he recognized. It was one of the most popular songs from the band on his t-shirt.

Man, he's pretty good. The rhythm Miguel was tapping out was a bit complex, but he seemed to do it with ease. All of a sudden, a thought popped into Tommy's head.

"Hey, Theo! Come listen to this!"

Theo pushed his glasses up his nose, peered over at Tommy and got up. He moseyed over and stood near Miguel, listening. Miguel stopped immediately, embarrassed by the attention.

"No, keep playing, man! Theo is a drummer!" Tommy encouraged.

"You like to play drums?" Miguel asked, staring up at Theo.

"More than almost anything else. You too?"

Miguel smiled. He began tapping out the song again. Theo nodded in beat.

Tommy foraged around in the grass until he found what he was looking for: a long, skinny stick. He snapped it in half, and then half again. He handed the four makeshift drum sticks to the two musicians, who began to play.

"Your name's Theo?" Miguel inquired.

"Yep. And you're..."

Tommy jumped in proudly. "This is Miguel." *I should have introduced them earlier!* thought Tommy. *It would have made getting to know Miguel so much easier to have someone else around who had something in common with him.*

Tommy began to hum the melody and pretty soon, the boys were laughing and belting out the chorus with everybody else joining in. Tommy looked over at Miguel, who looked way more comfortable than ever before. Music was something they could all understand without even trying.

The song gradually gave way to silence, and all that could be heard in the distance was the beautiful afternoon thunderstorm. Tommy sat back, contented. Theo and Miguel were deep in conversation; probably about drumming, or music, or the band, or maybe something else entirely.

12 Greetings and Introductions

"Hey, Theo! Miguel! We should play at my house sometime. I can bring my microphone, and Theo, you can bring your drums set so Miguel can try it out. Maybe we can even record something together!"

"Yes!" said Miguel, louder than Tommy had ever heard him talk. "Back at home, my friends and I used to make the craziest music videos."

Theo jumped at the idea, and in no time, the three boys were busy planning a jam session at Tommy's house. It was almost as if, without noticing, Tommy and Miguel and Theo had been friends for a long time.

And he wasn't just a new friend, he was one of them. Tommy grinned just thinking about it. *This could be the beginning of something really cool*, he thought.

Just the beginning...

Day 2   ART OF THE HEART®

1. Write **See, Smile, Step, Shake, Speak** on the board and have students repeat several times.

2. Invite a student up to the front and demonstrate:
   SEE- make eye contact
   SMILE- as you look the person in the eyes
   STEP- toward the person or lean in a little, if you are already close
   SHAKE- palm to palm and firm (but not so firm that you hurt the other person!)
   SPEAK- "It's nice to meet you!" and then ask a question

3. Pair up the students and have them practice.

4. Pass out activity sheets and have students cut out the five rectangles.

5. Have them mix them up on their desks and put in order several times.

You'll Need:
- See, Smile, Step, Shake, Speak! activity sheet
- Scissors

Day 3   WRITING FROM THE HEART

Ask your students to consider the following journal prompt and answer it according to your classroom writing requirements:

Is it easy or hard for you to meet new people? Give an example.

You'll Need:
- Greetings and Introductions activity sheet (1/student)

Days 2-5

Day 4 CREATIVE CONNECTION

1. Begin the lesson with a discussion, using the following questions and answers:
   - *What is a "first impression"?*
     The first thing you think about after you meet a new person.
   - *How do we make a bad first impression?*
     Not look at someone who is speaking with you.
     Talk only about yourself and don't ask the other person questions.
     Act as though you are more concerned about looking cool, smart, or important, than making the other person feel good.
   - *What does it mean to make a good first impression?*
     You show excitement about meeting the other person.
     You show the other person they are important by asking them questions.
     The other person feels better when they leave you.

2. Remember: Sometimes first impressions are wrong. We might think a person is mean the first time we meet them, but this is not how they really are. It is important to get to know other kids and give them a second chance!

3. Pass out the activity sheets and discuss when students have completed the work.

You'll Need:
- Five Steps to Making a GOOD First Impression! activity sheet
- Pencils

Day 5 TECH TIME

Interactive Whiteboard Activity on MyManners Portal

Help the stars of Merryville figure out the missing steps to a great greeting!

MANNERS IN ACTION

Whooooo will hang the **Happle** this week?

FRIENDLINESS—Welcoming others by offering a quick smile and a kind word
MATURITY—The ability to make the right choice in spite of negative influences

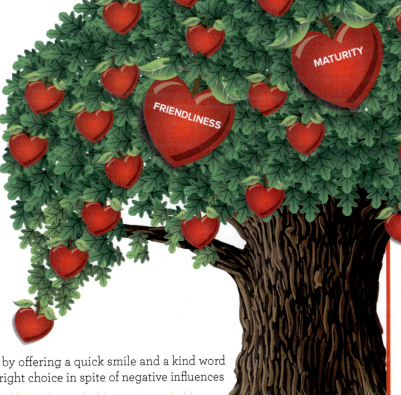

WEEK 13
ENCOURAGING CONVERSATION

Big Ideas

- Conversations are an opportunity to connect with others.
- If you're talking, you're not learning.
- We show others how much we care for and respect them by the way we participate in conversations.

For Your Heart

We can hardly remember our world without cell phones and computers or texting and emailing. Our thumbs and fingers have replaced our mouths and ears as transmitters and receivers of information. Our words are spell-checked and auto-corrected. We "talk" in phrases rather than complete sentences.

Beyond these obvious struggles, did you know that only 7% of communication takes place in words, while 38% is through tone and pitch of voice and 55% is visual? When someone reads a text or email from us, they are actually only getting 7% of what we are trying to communicate! They are reading our words without the added benefit of seeing our eyes and our body language, without hearing the inflection and emphasis in our voice. No wonder we have an epidemic of miscommunication!

The opportunity to develop good listening skills is lost in electronic communication, making it hard to experience the give and take of meaningful conversation.

For the Hearts of Your Students

Of all the life lessons you have the privilege of teaching your students, this one ranks near the top in importance. The ability to engage effectively in conversation is a skill that enables learning, protects against isolation, and encourages participation in the world.

What a privilege it is to help your students master the art of conversation! The next Winston Churchill, Susan B. Anthony, or Martin Luther King, Jr. may be sitting in your classroom this year. Children who learn the give-and-take of conversing become better students, friends, and citizens.

In this week's lesson, you'll teach your students to use *self-control* as they learn to be good listeners. Through face-to-face practice, you'll encourage *participation* in conversation that enables your students to connect with each other and the world around them.

13 Encouraging Conversation

SELF-CONTROL—The ability to manage yourself when no one is looking

PARTICIPATION—Choosing to be fully involved in the task or project at hand

REMEMBER

SKILLS AND OBJECTIVES

- Children will learn to respectfully converse by continuing the topic of the discussion.
- Children will learn to encourage others through words.
- Children will learn to encourage others through body language.

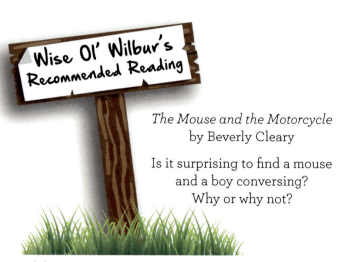

The Mouse and the Motorcycle by Beverly Cleary

Is it surprising to find a mouse and a boy conversing? Why or why not?

GUIDING CHILDREN'S LEARNING

1. Begin the lesson by introducing the *Heart Attributes* for the week, SELF-CONTROL and PARTICIPATION.

2. It's Story Time! Read aloud or listen to the recording of **One on One**

3. After the story, lead your students in the following discussion:
   - *Who are the three main characters in this story?*
   Guiming, Wesley and Ol' McDonald
   - *What do Guiming and Wesley have in common?*
   They both love basketball!
   - *How has Wesley been inconsiderate to Guiming lately?*
   He's been late and has not apologized
   - *How does it make Guiming feel when Wesley shows up late and says nothing?*
   Guiming is angry and frustrated.
   - *How does Guiming react to Wesley?*
   He fouls him and loses his temper.
   - *Who helped the boys realize what was going on underneath all the emotions?*
   Ol'McDonald
   - *What could the boys have done better?*
   They could have communicated better. Guiming should have told Wesley how much it bothered him that they were late. Wesley should have told Guiming how difficult his math homework had become lately.

MANNERS IN ACTION

1. Review the definitions of the *Heart Attributes*, SELF-CONTROL and PARTICIPATION.

2. Discuss these *Big Ideas* with your students:
   - Conversation is learning how to discuss different ideas with others.
   - We can encourage conversation with our words.
   - We can encourage conversation with our body language.

3. How can we show SELF-CONTROL and PARTICIPATION this week? Having conversations with others can sometimes feel very difficult, but if we practice participating in conversations and paying attention to what is being said, we can encourage others that we really want to be their friend! It is important to think carefully about the situation and the person so that we can connect with them. Look for someone that you don't normally speak with and have a good conversation with them.

Day 1

ONE ON ONE

Once upon a heart in Merryville, it was the second day in a row that Wesley was late. Mumbling angrily, Guiming threw the basketball against the park fence. He spun around in circles, hoping for any glimpse of his lanky, new friend to round the corner or cut through the woods.

When Guiming and Wesley first met, they didn't seem to have much in common. In fact, Wesley had been one of the boys that had teased him when he first came to school. It wasn't until Wesley had mentioned his favorite NBA player that Guiming realized how much they both loved basketball. They could quote to each other, completely from memory, the last decade of NBA champions, compare all the stars from the past with their favorite new recruits, and they were a dead-even match on the court.

The two had agreed to meet at the public court after school several days a week. And the last two times, Wesley had been late. Guiming hadn't said much, but inside, he was furious.

Finally, a half an hour late, Wesley strolled past the turn in the lane, down the park path and through the open gate. He seemed cheerful and called out, "Hey Gui, ready to shoot?"

Guiming replied with a stony silence and a stonier stare.

"Let's do this!" Wesley picked up the ball and started to dribble. As he closed in on the basket, Guiming fouled him, knocking him to the pavement.

"Chill out," Wesley said, scoffing. He picked up the ball, went up for another shot and Guiming fouled him again, batting the ball away.

"What's your deal?" yelled Wesley, his face turning red.

"Yeah, like you have no idea!" said Guiming.

"Uh, because I don't. You don't have to be—"

"Don't have to be what?" Guiming countered.

"Seriously, hold on. What's wrong?"

"Wesley! You've been late every day this week!"

"You don't have to get all mad."

"Yeah, like I don't have a right to be mad."

"If you're gonna be like this, I don't wanna play," Wesley snapped, as he started to leave.

"Fine. Go!" Guiming yelled, storming off the other way.

Guiming's blood was boiling and his breath was coming in short, shallow whiffs as he stomped out of the park. He didn't even say sorry!

Eventually, Guiming's breathing slowed and he stopped to think as the minutes crawled by. Wesley had become one of Guiming's best friends in Merryville and now they had just gotten into a huge fight.

"Oh, alright, alright," he grumbled, turning to follow Wesley.

He walked past several driveways until he heard faint voices in the distance. At the corner of Ol' McDonald's property, Guiming recognized the voices of Wesley and Ol' McDonald and stopped not far from them behind a clump of trees.

"...he was just super mean," he heard Wesley saying.

There was a long pause. Ol' McDonald must be thinking. When you talked to the farmer, he always spent a lot of the conversation gazing deep into your eyes and musing.

"And," Wesley went on hotly, "I mean, what did I do to him? I wasn't intentionally late."

"What kept you?"

Guiming listened in rapt anticipation for the answer.

"I had more homework than I normally do. And he knows I'm bad at math so it takes me longer."

"I'm sorry Guiming's response was so hurtful," Ol' McDonald comforted. "It sounds like he really cares about your time together."

Guiming smiled. No one in town knew how to put things better than Ol' McDonald.

"I know and I... and I do too. It's just that..." Wesley paused for the right words.

"You missed each other today. You didn't connect. He didn't understand you and you didn't understand him."

"Exactly!" Wesley exclaimed. "That's it...we missed each other! I had no idea he was even upset before today, and then everything just exploded!"

"And he had no idea why you were late, because you didn't tell him."

"I guess not," Guiming heard Wesley admit. He could hear the tone of remorse.

13 Encouraging Conversation

"Wesley," Ol' McDonald said softly. When Ol' McDonald said your name in that deep, tender voice of his, you knew he was going to ask a question that would cut right through you.

"Wesley, why do you think he was upset that you were late?"

"Well, maybe he's got better things to do."

"I'm not so sure that's the whole of it," Ol' McDonald countered.

"I... well, I don't really know."

Guiming couldn't wait any longer. He rounded the corner. He expected them to both be surprised to see him, but only Wesley seemed taken aback.

"I'm sorry, I wasn't trying to eavesdrop. I just wanted to say, I'm sorry, Wesley."

"Oh, I..." Wesley said, not sure what to say next.

"Wes, I'm sorry about today. I just love basketball," Guiming continued.

Wesley smiled warmly.

"And you're like..." Guiming said, trying to sound tougher than he felt. "Like the only person who can come close to beating me."

Wesley laughed, "Come close? Please. I beat you every time."

The two boys wrapped each other in a hug. They looked around for the old farmer. He was off by himself, gardening or weeding or doing whatever Ol' McDonald did on days like that (something no one in Merryville knew exactly). He stood up, brushed his hands off and waved to the two boys. Sometimes, Ol' McDonald's silence said more than most people's words.

Just the beginning...

Day 2   MUSIC OF THE HEART®

1. Hand out activity sheets and take turns reading the conversation starters aloud.
2. Explain that conversation starters do not usually have yes or no answers and that we are showing our friends that we are interested in what's going on with them!
3. Have students come up with two original starters and then share them.
4. Sharing can happen in groups of two or three. Encourage the conversations to continue beyond the initial answers to the questions.
5. This is a time when it's okay to talk quietly in class!

You'll Need:
- **Let's Get Started!** activity sheet (1/student)
- Pencils

Day 3   WRITING FROM THE HEART

Ask your students to consider the following journal prompt and answer it according to your classroom writing requirements:

What do you most LOVE talking about? Tell us more!

You'll Need:
- **Encouraging Conversation** activity sheet (1/student)

Days 2-5

Day 4 CREATIVE CONNECTION

Today, we are practicing conversation starters so that we get really, really good at it.

You'll Need:
- Squishy Ball

1. Have students sit in a circle on the floor.

2. Have one student ask another student an open-ended question (these are not Yes or No questions) and then toss them the ball.

3. After catching the ball, the student answers, asks another student a question, and then tosses the ball.

4. Each toss must be to a different person until everyone has had a turn to answer and ask a question.

5. Another version of this game is to try to keep a relatively stream-lined conversation going as the ball is tossed from one student to another. This happens when the student answers a question, makes a statement and then asks another student something related or along the same lines. It's fun to see what the children come up with and to see how long they can keep it going!

I was born in Tennessee, where were you born?
I was born in Maine, but I really didn't like the cold. Is it cold where you were born?
No. I'm from Louisiana, but I wish it would snow more often. Then, we could ski! Is skiing hard?
I don't know. I've never skied before, but I love playing football. Who is your favorite football team?
I like the Patriots! Do you know where the Patriots are from? etc.

Day 5 TECH TIME

Interactive Whiteboard Activity on MyManners Portal

Test your knowledge of conversations with this exciting game board!

MANNERS IN ACTION

*Whooooo will hang the **Happle** this week?*

SELF-CONTROL—The ability to manage yourself when no one is looking
PARTICIPATION—Choosing to be fully involved in the task or project at hand

89

WEEK 14
USING THE PHONE

Big Ideas

- Phone manners are much more than learning how to make and take calls.

- Children gain responsibility in other areas of life when they learn to use the phone responsibly.

- Learning how and when to use the phone protects children from the risk of overuse and addiction.

For Your Heart

Phones have come a long way. No longer just designed for calls, phones are used for texting, picture taking, searching the Internet, and so much more.

According to Pew Research, 95% of Americans own a cell phone. 77% own a smart phone. Even 25% of 6 to 9 year olds own a cell phone and that number jumps to 60% of 10 to 14 year olds. How often do we use them? Adults and teens check their phones 150 times per day (every six minutes) and send an average of 110 texts per day.

Most teens are on their phones all the time—in school, in bed at night, while others are talking to them, and while they are trying to do their homework. It has become increasingly difficult for parents to set enforceable rules.

Parents often say that one of he greatest struggles they face today is how to mange their child's screen time, particularly the phone.

For the Hearts of Your Students

Helping your students develop good phone manners in today's world includes teaching traditional phone etiquette, as well as teaching how and when to use the phone.

In this week's lesson, teaching your students how to answer a phone, make calls, take messages, and how to carry on a pleasant phone conversation, are opportunities to instill *courtesy* toward others. Helping children understand the need to identify themselves when calling a friend's house, or to speak slowly and clearly into the phone, teaches children how to think of others ahead of themselves.

Responsibility in phone use is a good place to start with your students. Instilling good phone habits in your young students will enable them to have control over their phones so their phones don't take control over them as they get older.

14 Using the Phone

RESPONSIBILITY—Following through on your duties without supervision

COURTESY—Respectful and well-mannered words and actions toward others

REMEMBER

SKILLS AND OBJECTIVES

- Children will discuss phone courtesy.
- Children will learn when and where cell phone use is permissible.
- Children will learn when and where cell phone use is inappropriate.

Cell Phoney
by Julia Cook

Do you agree with the rules of cell phone usage? How could they be improved?

GUIDING CHILDREN'S LEARNING

1. Begin the lesson by introducing the *Heart Attributes* for the week, RESPONSIBILITY and COURTESY.

2. It's Story Time! Read aloud or listen to the recording of **Getting to Know You**

3. After the story, lead your students in the following discussion:
   - *How do Sarah and Allie spend most of their time?*
     Texting and talking on the phone.
   - *What do Sarah and Allie really know about one another?*
     Not too much, because they rarely spend time just being together.
   - *What did Sarah's dad help her with?*
     He helped Sarah restore the bicycle so she could ride over to Allie's house. He helped her see that she needed to spend time with Allie getting to know her.
   - *Why did Sarah leave Allie's house so quickly?*
     She was realizing how little they talked and visited and she grew frustrated.
   - *Why did Sarah crash on her bicycle?*
     She was looking at her phone and lost control of the bike. What did Sarah's dad mean when he said, "You have to be with someone." Perhaps looking at them in the eyes, talking heart to heart, sharing experiences with them.
   - *What did Sarah's dad mean when he said, "You have to be with someone"?*
     Perhaps looking at them in the eyes, talking heart to heart, sharing experiences with them.

MANNERS IN ACTION

1. Review the definitions of the *Heart Attributes*, RESPONSIBILITY and COURTESY.

2. Discuss these *Big Ideas* with your students:
   - *Learning correct phone use is part of the RESPONSIBILITY of using a phone.*
   - *There are certain times and places when cell phone use is not COURTEOUS.*
   - *There are certain times and places when cell phone use is acceptable.*

3. *How can we show RESPONSIBILITY and COURTESY this week? What times and places do you feel we should not use a phone? When you are spending time with friends or family, it is important that you don't use the phone unless you absolutely have to. Giving all your attention to your company shows them respect! Let's keep that in mind this week, as we explore the other important manners we ought to have when using the telephone.*

Day 1

GETTING TO KNOW YOU

Once upon a heart in Merryville, Sarah and Allie made quite a pair. The two girls could rarely be found apart. Sarah felt honored when Allie invited her over the first time. The only downside was how far across town they lived from each other. They made up for it, however, by texting all the time.

Normally, Sarah hated talking on the phone, but when Allie called, they would chat for hours on end about things they both loved. Everyone knew that Sarah and Allie were becoming best friends.

One day, Sarah got an idea. She saved up and bought the cheapest, rustiest bike she could find. Her dad brought out a large coffee can of oil, a couple of screwdrivers and wrenches and went to work. He showed Sarah how to fill the tires with air, how to remove the chain to soak it in oil and how to sand off and paint over the rusty spots.

"So... tell me a little about Allie," her dad said as they worked.

Sarah paused. "Well, I mean, she's pretty cool."

"I gathered that much," her dad laughed. "Tell me about her. What is she like?"

"She's nice." Sarah didn't really know what to say. She felt annoyed that she was unable to come up with anything off the top of her head.

"You two text all the time. Surely you must have something."

Sarah thought for a long time. She couldn't really remember what they texted about. It seemed like they just texted and talked, but she couldn't really recall anything about Allie.

"What do you two talk about?"

"I don't know... just stuff." Sarah was wracking her brain for something real and deep to say, but nothing came. It surprised and disappointed her that for how much they texted, they didn't say much.

"Hey, look at that! Good as new!" her dad said, motioning to the bike.

Sarah was still a little annoyed as she rode to Allie's. She was so distracted that, as she sat on the couch with her best friend, she was hardly aware of her phone. Allie sat next to her, laughing every now and then at something she read or watched on her phone. Over and over again, she heard the soft Bzzz and Allie would swipe open a new text.

They hadn't talked much since Sarah had arrived. This wasn't out of the ordinary, because they were usually both on their phones. Something, however, was not sitting right with Sarah.

"Allie," she said hopefully.

"Yep?" Allie didn't look up. She was texting at least three other people.

"Hey, Allie," she said again, trying to get the other girl's full attention.

"What's up? Hold on, just a second." Smiling at something she was reading, Allie didn't look up.

Sarah got impatient, "I'm gonna' head out."

"Aww, ok," Allie said, a little disappointed. She stopped typing to hug Sarah quickly, but then went right back to her phone.

Sarah was in a sour mood when she kicked up the stand, swung her leg over the bike and started the ride home. She was about halfway home when she noticed that her phone kept buzzing. She picked it out of her pocket with great effort and steered with one hand. It was a little shaky, but she thought it might be Allie texting her.

Before she knew it, she felt the front wheel jerk to the right. Her hands slipped up and over the handlebars and the whole bike - girl and all - crashed to the pavement. Her phone went skittering across the ground.

Sarah was so angry, she actually screamed. Her phone screen was almost completely ruined, a total web of cracks. The knuckles on both her hands and one knee were skinned and bleeding and stung fiercely.

Once she was back at home, her dad bandaged her up and asked, "What's wrong, Sarah? You seem upset about more than just the cuts."

Sarah thought for a moment. "I really like Allie, and I really do want to get to know her for real, but I guess after you and I talked, I realized that we mainly just text and stuff."

Her dad nodded, understanding. "I'm sorry."

"I think she's so awesome, Dad. I really do."

"You know, using your phone is actually a lot like riding your bike."

Sarah was confused. She squinted at her dad skeptically.

"No, I'm serious," her dad laughed. "Bikes can get us places faster. Phones help us communicate faster. And it's fun. Riding bikes and using phones is fun, but it can be dangerous, too. You have to be careful when you use them...careful to obey the rules, and careful to pay attention, because they can easily get the better of you."

14 Using the Phone

Sarah had to think about this for a while.

Her dad continued, "Sometimes, when you really want to get to know someone, you have to just be with them. When you're with them, you can see the whole person. Texting or talking on the phone should never take the place of just being with that person. Sometimes phones can help us get to know a friend, but sometimes our phones become more important than our friends and end up doing more harm than good."

Her dad turned to walk away, smiled and left Sarah to ponder it all. Nervously, bike trembling a bit more than usual, Sarah rode back to Allie's house. She stuffed her phone into her pocket, parked the bike on the curb and walked up to the door. Allie opened it, as she was about to knock.

"Hey," Allie said happily, "you're back!"

"Hey," Sarah smiled, "I just wanted to see you."

Just the beginning...

Day 2   ART OF THE HEART®

1. Discuss with your students the ever-increasing presence of cell phones in daily life.

2. Although there are many advantages to cell phones, there are some disadvantages as well.
   - Cell phones often distract us from actually engaging with the people that we are with.
   - Cell phones may also distract us from concentrating on an important task at hand. An example of this is texting and driving!

3. Give the **NO PHONE ZONE! #1** activity sheets to the students and ask them to describe each situation depicted in the pictures.

4. When students have completed the activity sheet, discuss why these particular situations are NO PHONE ZONES.

5. Ask your students to name other NO PHONE ZONES!

You'll Need:
- **NO PHONE ZONE! #1** activity sheet
- Pencils

Day 3   WRITING FROM THE HEART

Ask your students to consider the following journal prompt and answer it according to your classroom writing requirements:

Describe a time you wished someone was paying attention to you rather than to their phone.

You'll Need:
- **Using the Phone** activity sheet (1/student)

Days 2-5

Day 4 CREATIVE CONNECTION

1. Here's a chance for your students to create a NO PHONE ZONE! sign and start their own campaign for wise cell phone use.

2. Have each student create an original sign.

3. When all signs have been completed, post them on a bulletin board and have a closed-ballot contest so students can vote on the most effective sign.

4. Award the winner(s) with publicity of their sign throughout the school.

You'll Need:
- NO PHONE ZONE! #2 activity sheet
- Crayons

Day 5 TECH TIME

Interactive Whiteboard Activity on MyManners Portal

A world without phones?! Can you imagine?!

MANNERS IN ACTION

Whooooo will hang the **Happle** this week?

RESPONSIBILITY— Following through on your duties without supervision
COURTESY—Respectful and well-mannered words and actions toward others

WEEK 15
WRITING FROM THE HEART

Big Ideas

- Writing a thoughtful sentiment to someone without expectation of return shows how much you care.

- The more dependent we become on electronic communication, the more important handwritten communication becomes.

- Learning to express feelings and thoughts on paper opens the imagination for critical thinking and creative writing.

For Your Heart

Why is it important to master the art of handwritten correspondence in this text-savvy, modern high-tech world? Look at these statistics:

- 95% of emails are never opened. (With 2.5 billion social networking users in the world, that's a lot of thoughts and words that never reach the intended recipient.)
- 44% of junk mail is thrown away unopened.
- 99.2% of hand-written notes *are* opened.

Can you imagine *not* opening a hand-written note or letter? When someone takes the time to write by hand in lieu of a quick text message or email, it expresses more than words alone can say. The hand-written note becomes the hug, the smile, or the handshake you would receive in person.

Challenge yourself this week to write words from your heart along with your students. The recipients of your thoughtfulness will be most appreciative.

For the Hearts of Your Students

Encouraging your students to write letters will improve their ability to communicate, increase their social skills and support the mastery of writing skills.

In this week's lesson, you'll help your students learn the significance of written communication and the special place it holds in building relationships as they practice being *thoughtful* and *expressive* in their letter writing.

You can be a part of bringing the return of the hand-written note by instilling a love of pencil to paper in your students, even in our fast-paced, electronic world. Studies show that creative thinking and problem-solving skills are heightened in the process of forming letters and words by hand. Thoughts expressed on paper linger in the mind and heart and ignite the imagination.

15 Writing from the Heart

THOUGHTFUL—Looking for ways to make others feel loved

EXPRESSIVE—Revealing the content of your heart

REMEMBER

SKILLS AND OBJECTIVES

- Children will learn to recognize appropriate times to communicate through writing.
- Children will learn how to encourage others through writing.
- Children will learn to express their feelings through a written letter.

Charlotte's Web by E.B. White

How did Charlotte communicate? Can she be described as thoughtful and expressive?

GUIDING CHILDREN'S LEARNING

1. Begin the lesson by introducing this week's *Heart Attributes*: THOUGHTFUL and EXPRESSIVE. Review the definitions throughout the week.

2. Let's Listen! Read aloud or play the recording of **My Dear Florence**

3. After the story, lead your students in the following discussion questions:
   - *What project did Emma help Florence with?*
     Planting the gardens in downtown Merryville.
   - *How did Emma and Florence feel about their work?*
     It was hard work, but they enjoyed it and loved looking at the flowers.
   - *How do you know Emma cared about the flowers after the day she planted them?*
     She went by often to check on them and to chase away the rabbit.
   - *How was the garden destroyed?*
     An unexpected freeze came and wiped out all the flowers.
   - *How did Emma know Florence was sad about the lost plants?*
     She saw her crying.
   - *Why did Emma decide to write to Florence?*
     She remembered all the times her dad had written to her and how he was always able to touch her heart with his words.
   - *Have you ever written to someone when you didn't know exactly what to say out loud?* (Answers will vary.)

MANNERS IN ACTION

1. At the end of the discussion, point out the **Happle Tree** and how the number of **Happles** is growing. Remind your students that their hearts are growing as well! Did they hear the *Heart Attributes*, THOUGHTFUL and EXPRESSIVE, in the story?

2. Discuss these *Big Ideas*:
   - *There are times when writing to someone is even more special than speaking with them.*
   - *I can encourage others when I write to them.*
   - *EXPRESSING my feelings through a letter or a note shows someone how special they are to me.*

3. Ask your children to think about people in their lives who would like to receive a note or a card from them. Ask them to think about reasons a written thought can sometimes be even more meaningful than a spoken one. Who can they write to this week?

Day 1

MY DEAR FLORENCE

Once upon a heart in Merryville, Emma's hands were covered in fluffy black dirt. There was even a smudge that streaked across her forehead. A sharp little pain in the small of her back ached and clamored for her attention.

It's worth it, Emma sighed to herself. She lifted off the straw hat that had been protecting her from the sun. The cool breeze ran through her hair. She looked over at Florence.

"Isn't it beautiful?"

"Almost unspeakably," Florence nodded.

Before them, in an intricate swirl, flamed a rainbow of freshly planted flowers, marking the end of Main Street. It spilled out in all directions with flowers more vibrant than Emma had ever seen.

Everyone in Merryville admired the flowers on Main Street. They were the "can't miss" attraction of downtown that brought a smile to even the grumpiest face.

For Emma, there was something hypnotizing about planting flowers. They nestled into the dirt in their little beds of soil, all tucked in by the gloved hands of a gardener, and then, like a child waking up on Christmas morning, they stretched their limbs every which way and pushed up into the sun.

Grateful for having been chosen to assist Florence this year, Emma said, "Job well done, huh, Miss Florence?"

"Oh, Emma, yes, yes! Job well done, my sweet bud!"

Emma came back every day to check on their progress. She knew each petal by heart, and noticed a broken stem here or a trampled spot there. Once she waited for hours for a glimpse of a pesky rabbit, so she could chase him away from nibbling on the new green leaves.

A few weeks after planting day, Emma was shocked to wake up to a thick layer of frost on her window panes and her thoughts went immediately to the freshly planted flowers. This was not right! She and Florence had planned so carefully. They had waited until winter was fully over before planting, but when she came down for cocoa with her dad, she learned that a hard freeze had come quickly and unexpectedly during the night. On her way to school, Emma walked down Main Street and stopped dead in her tracks. It was a wasteland. The heavy frost had beaten down the flowers and left them helpless and broken. Their heads hung low. She couldn't believe her eyes.

She heard Florence slip in softly beside her. Emma looked up and saw the glimmer of a tear in the woman's eyes. Emma wanted to cry herself.

"It's…" no words came from Emma's mouth, even though her heart was overflowing with emotion. Florence opened her mouth, but quickly let it drop closed.

"It's…" Emma tried again, "I've got to go to school."

Quickly, she spun around and ran off. It wasn't normal for the two to part without a hug, but today was not a normal day. Long days of hard work had been lost, and without warning, their garden was destroyed.

Emma knew she needed to say something to Miss Florence. And yet, when she imagined herself speaking with her, she could not come up with any of the right words.

Then, she thought of her father. Every year on her birthday, he would give her a special book and write a note on the inside cover. What he wrote were some of the most cherished words she had ever read. They had the brightness of his love and an echo of truth in them because he knew her so well. She took out a pen and some paper, hoping she could write what was in her heart.

Dearest Florence… She had read that in fancy books. It didn't seem right.

Hey, Miss Florence! That wasn't right either. It didn't fit the mood.

She put the pen down. The words seemed like fish in an aquarium, she could catch glimpses of their color and their life, but she could never quite reach out and grasp them. Emma thought about her dad again.

What she loved about her father was that he chose words he knew fit her. They were Emma-words and when he gave them to her, it felt like he gave her things she could hold and smell and cradle. Emma finally decided on, *My Dear Miss Florence*.

Somehow those words seemed to fit her friend, so she began crafting the letter, pressing her feelings directly into the ink on the blank page. When she was finished, Emma smiled. She meant every word.

The next day, she found Florence at the flower beds, kneeling down and gazing at the skeletal plants, no doubt making plans for next year. She glanced up as Emma walked to her and smiled with hope in her eyes.

"I wrote you something." Emma handed her the letter.

Florence took the letter, hugged Emma close, and said, "Thank you, my sweet bud. Now you remember, all will be well." Nodding, Emma walked away, while Florence sat down on a nearby bench to read her letter.

15 Writing from the Heart

My Dear Miss Florence,
I didn't know what to say when I saw tears in your eyes. I knew you were sad for the people who won't have flowers to make them smile. Miss Florence, you remind me of spring and you always make me smile. I just wanted to tell you that I want to help you when you decide to plant new flowers in our garden.
Love,

Your Emma

When Emma looked back over her shoulder, she saw Florence smiling as she read Emma's letter over and over again. *Sometimes,* Emma thought, *I can write what I feel, better than I can say it. Sometimes, writing is the best way of all to tell someone what I want them to hear.*

Just the beginning...

Day 2   MUSIC OF THE HEART®

1. As the students come in, play the song, "Please, Mr. Postman."
2. Ask them how often they get letters or cards in the mail and how it makes them feel.
3. Discuss why it is important to send handwritten cards and letters to special people in our lives:
    - Letters and cards show you care about the recipient, even when they are far away.
    - Letters show that you are willing to take the time to do something special for someone.
    - Handwriting is personal and fun.
    - Letters can be written on special stationery.
4. What should I say in a letter or a card?
    - Tell a little about yourself – what you have been doing or thinking about lately.
    - Share some of your thoughts or ideas.
    - Ask questions so the person receiving it has the opportunity to write you back.
    - Express your feelings in a clear and respectful way.
    - Sign the letter, "Love," "Respectfully," or "With Love."
5. Ask students to think of someone at home who would appreciate a special letter.
6. Students will write and send letters home by the end of the week.

You'll Need:
- *Please, Mr. Postman* by The Marvelettes https://www.youtube.com/watch?v=rG-JcbHni4rc

Day 3   WRITING FROM THE HEART

1. Give students the activity sheet and lined paper. Have them begin a letter on lined paper including the date, salutation, body and closing.
2. Remind your students of thoughts and ideas they can include in a letter that were discussed on Day 2. If students need more time, this exercise can be completed on Day 4.

You'll Need:
- **Model Letter and Envelope** activity sheet
- Lined paper and pencils

Days 2-5

Day 4 CREATIVE CONNECTION

1. Have students complete the letters they began on Day 3.
2. Check for spelling and punctuation.
3. Check for the correct date, salutation and closing.
4. Give each student an envelope and have them address it with their home address.
5. Stamp and send the letters home.
6. Over the next week, ask your students if the letters were received and how the recipients responded!

You'll Need:
- Model Letter and Envelope activity sheet from Day 3 (1/student)
- Letters from Day 3
- Stamped envelopes (1/student)

Day 5 TECH TIME

Interactive Whiteboard Activity on MyManners Portal

Help Sketch apologize to Henry properly! He's a first timer!

MANNERS IN ACTION

Whooooo will hang the **Happle** this week?

THOUGHTFUL—Looking for ways to make others feel loved
EXPRESSIVE—Revealing the content of your heart

WEEK 16
RESPECTING ADULTS

Big Ideas

- Honor and respect for parents and other adults is shown by responding politely and promptly to requests and questions.

- Answering adults with respect is always the right thing to do.

- Adults make rules to protect children from harm, not to spoil their fun.

For Your Heart

Regardless of how little respect your students have for other adults in their lives, when they enter your classroom you can command their respect through your words, demeanor and actions. The fewer admirable role models your students have to look up to, the easier it is for you to become the one adult they trust and accept.

Your students are looking for someone who will:

- Always tell the truth.
- Set boundaries and enforce consequences.
- Maintain the same temperament from one day to the next.

Your students may come from an environment where adults break more promises than they keep, but a teacher who keeps his word wins the fervent respect of the students. Teachers who establish boundaries and enforce consequences change the behavior and consequently, the lives of their students. Finally, the teacher who is even-tempered and whose responses are predictable and calm is the teacher who becomes a trusted advocate and life-long counselor.

On the days when students try your patience and press every button they know to press, it is difficult to maintain peace and rationale, but keep in mind that you are setting the example. In those times, remind yourself that teachers who lead by example train students who become leaders.

For the Hearts of Your Students

For your students to grow into respectable adults, they must first learn to earn respect by giving respect to adults. By your example, your classroom can become one of calm cooperation that positions your students for success.

In this week's lesson, you have the charge of teaching your students to show *honor* to authority figures. Encouraging *obedience* in your students leads to the development of character that will enable them to become leaders in their school and community.

It has been said, "Children develop character by what they see, by what they hear and by what they are repeatedly led to do."

16 Respecting Adults

HONOR—Valuing the worth of another by showing respect

OBEDIENCE—Choosing to submit to authority

REMEMBER

SKILLS AND OBJECTIVES

- Children will learn why it is important to honor adults.
- Children will learn how to show respect to people in authority.
- Children will learn appropriate titles for leaders and dignitaries.

Pippi Longstocking by Astrid Lindgren

What heart attributes would you use to describe Pippi? Do you think she is respectful toward adults?

GUIDING CHILDREN'S LEARNING

1. Begin the lesson by introducing the *Heart Attributes* for the week, HONOR and OBEDIENCE.

2. It's Story Time! Read aloud or listen to the recording of *I Don't Understand!*

3. After the story, lead your students in the following discussion:
   - *Evelyn makes a lot of mistakes in this story. To whom did Evelyn show disrespect?*
   Her mother, the crossing guard, her teacher and her coach.
   - *Was Evelyn showing HONOR and OBEDIENCE for adults by her actions? What WAS she showing?*
   She was showing selfishness and disrespect.
   - *What did Evelyn continue to say?*
   "I don't understand why everyone keeps being mean to me!"
   - *Were the adults really being mean to her? What was happening?*
   They were concerned for Evelyn's well-being. Even though she did not agree with the adults, Evelyn should have treated them with HONOR and OBEDIENCE.
   - *How did Wilbur help Evelyn?*
   Wilbur recommended Evelyn respond with respect toward adults and remember they want to help her.

MANNERS IN ACTION

1. Review the definitions of the *Heart Attributes*, HONOR and OBEDIENCE.

2. Discuss these *Big Ideas*:
   - We must show respect for those in authority even when we disagree with them.
   - We should use the correct titles for those in authority or for dignitaries.
   - Showing HONOR and OBEDIENCE toward adults will help us in school and at home.

3. *What are some of the words and actions you can use to show adults that you HONOR and respect them?* Challenge the students to think about the way they interact with the adults in their lives. Ask them to give you specific examples of what they will do this week to show that they understand how important this is.

104

Day 1

I DON'T UNDERSTAND!

Once upon a heart in Merryville, Evelyn woke up and got dressed for school. Her mother called her to breakfast, but rather than coming to the kitchen, she decided to play a video game. Her mother called again, but she didn't answer. Finally, Evelyn's mother appeared at the door.

Peter and Penelope were in the tree outside Evelyn's window waiting to follow her to school and could overhear an unpleasant conversation. "Evelyn, it's time for breakfast," her mother said. "I made scrambled eggs and toast."

"I don't want eggs," yelled Evelyn. "You better work on your attitude, young lady," snapped her mother. "It's your attitude that's the problem, not mine," Evelyn snapped back.

Peter and Penelope couldn't believe what they were hearing. They scampered down the tree to wait for Evelyn. She came to the table without speaking to her mother or sister or brother. After taking just two bites, she pushed her plate away and jumped up from the table.

"I'm outta here," she barked. "Evelyn, you need to wait for your brother and sister," her mother reminded. But Evelyn was already out the door to school before her mother could stop her.

"Why is my mother always so mean to me?" Evelyn said out loud. "I don't understand." Peter and Penelope looked at each other nodding, "We understand."

Just a few blocks from her home, Evelyn came to the crosswalk in front of her school. PD and KC were playing with friends who were waiting for the crossing guard. But Evelyn didn't want to wait, because she wanted to be the first one to school. She darted out of the crowd and started running across the street. The crossing guard blew his whistle and shouted, "Evelyn, STOP!"

But Evelyn didn't stop. She looked back at him and kept running. He kept blowing the whistle. She kept running. PD and KC chased after her. When she got to the door of the school, she stopped and said to PD and KC, "Why does he blow the whistle ONLY at me? I don't understand." PD and KC looked at each other with a nod and said, "We understand."

Evelyn walked down the hall to her classroom. She sat down at her desk and started talking to Mary. Her teacher, Mr. Smith, said it was time to start the day, but Evelyn kept talking. He called her by name, but she didn't hear him, because she was still chattering away. Mr. Smith walked over and stood at her desk. She finally looked away from Mary and looked at him.

"Evelyn, you'll have to stay inside during recess, again," said Mr. Smith.

"Why do you always pick on me?" asked Evelyn. "I don't understand."

Because you're too busy talking. You don't listen," replied Mr. Smith. Turning to her classmates, Mr. Smith said, "Class, let's practice this week's word list."

Evelyn's day was busy with math problems and reading and lots of other stuff, but Evelyn stayed in trouble all day because she talked when she should have been listening.

Evelyn was glad when school ended and it was time for her soccer game. She really liked soccer. She was fast and had fun out-running the other kids. In today's game, the coach wanted everyone to have a chance to play. After a few minutes, he called Evelyn, Caroline, and Allie to the sidelines, but Evelyn ignored his call and kept playing. He called again, but she didn't listen. He called one more time and then asked the referee for a timeout to talk to Evelyn.

"Evelyn, you'll have to sit out the rest of the game for not listening," said the coach. "Until you can learn to listen to me and to be a team player, you can't play in the game." Evelyn kicked the dirt and pouted as she walked off the field. She didn't notice that Wilbur was watching from the trees. "Evvvvvvvelyyyyyn," Wilbur hooted. "Peter and Penelope said you might need my help. Come over here and let's talk."

"Wilbur," Evelyn began. "I don't understand why everybody is so mean to me."

"Whoooo's everybody?" asked Wilbur. "All the adults," answered Evelyn. "My mom, the crossing guard, Mr. Smith, and even my coach."

"Well, let's see," Wilbur said, as he put on his glasses. "Your mother fixed a good breakfast this morning, didn't she? The crossing guard tries to keep you safe, doesn't he? And I understand you'd rather talk than listen in class and at soccer."

"Well, I didn't want to stop playing my video game, but my mother made me come to the table, and I didn't like it. The crossing guard is too slow. Mr. Smith never lets us talk to our friends. And the coach wants to be fair to everybody, but I'm the best player," Evelyn snapped back.

"Well, Evelyn," answered Wilbur, "It seems to me your day would go a whole lot better if you showed adults a little respect. They have a hard time helping you when you don't respect them."

105

16 Respecting Adults

"But, Wilbur," Evelyn started. Wilbur interrupted, "Evelyn, just try giving them respect. That will change everything!" Evelyn went home mad at Wilbur and everyone else. But the more she thought about what Wilbur said, the more it made sense. Maybe there was something to the idea of respecting others that she was missing.

So the next day, Evelyn answered, "Yes, Ma'am" and came downstairs for breakfast the first time her mother called. Her mother was thankful for the new attitude. Evelyn felt better, too.

When Evelyn saw the crossing guard, she told him, "Good morning!" and waited for his signal before she crossed the street. She liked not hearing his whistle blow. Evelyn was the first one to answer, "Yes, Sir," when Mr. Smith was ready to start class. He noticed and smiled at her. Evelyn sat up taller in her desk.

All day long, Evelyn remembered what Wilbur told her about respecting adults. She couldn't believe how differently the adults treated her. At soccer practice, Evelyn even told her coach she was sorry about not listening the day before. She felt much better.

On her way home from soccer practice, Wilbur swooped down and said, "Evelyn, tell me about your day."

"Oh, Wilbur," Evelyn said. "I really tried to show respect all day long. And guess what? I had a great day!"

"Now, you understand," Wilbur said with a wink. "We have to respect others the way we want to be respected!"

Just the beginning...

Day 2 ART OF THE HEART®

1. Begin the lesson by reminding students that in previous grades they have learned to respect adults in their home, school, and community by following **Wilbur's Words of Wisdom**:
   - **A** Answer questions.
   - **D** Do what they say.
   - **U** Use their correct title.
   - **L** Listen and look them in the eye.
   - **T** Turn your frown upside down.
   - **S** Say "Sir" and "Ma'am."

2. Explain that today's lesson will be on showing respect for leaders in our government. Discuss:
   - *What does the word honor mean?*
     To respect, to obey, to say good things about someone
   - *Why should we honor the leaders of our country?*
     Because they are in charge of the people in our country
     Because honoring them shows respect for our country
   - *Should we honor leaders even if we don't agree with them?*
     Yes, because they have been elected to that office and we honor and respect the office.

3. Fill in the activity sheet by naming the leaders in your city, state and country.

You'll Need:
- **ADULTS** activity sheet
- Pencils

Day 3 WRITING FROM THE HEART

Ask your students to consider the following journal prompt and answer it according to your classroom writing requirements: *If you could meet any president from any time in history, who would you like to meet? What would you want to ask him?*

You'll Need:
- **Respecting Adults** activity sheet (1/student)

Days 2-5

Day 4 CREATIVE CONNECTION

1. Ask students to recall *Wilbur's Words of Wisdom* (see Day 2).
2. As a class, identify an elected official who will receive a **Thank You Note** from everyone in the class.
3. Have everyone cut out the **Thank You Note** and write a brief note of gratitude for his/her service.
4. Send the cards together in a large envelope.
5. Encourage your students that freely communicating with our elected officials is an important part of the rights and privileges we have as citizens of the United States of America. Every voice is important!

You'll Need:
- Thank You Note activity sheet
- Large envelope
- Postage

Day 5 TECH TIME

Interactive Whiteboard Activity on MyMannersPortal

Will you pass the pop Presidents Quiz?!

MANNERS IN ACTION

Whooooo will hang the **Happle** this week?

HONOR—Valuing the worth of another by showing respect
OBEDIENCE—Choosing to submit to authority

WEEK 17
RESPECTING THE TEAM

Big Ideas

- A cooperative spirit shows respect for team members through good sportsmanship and selfless interaction with others.

- Learning to cooperate, not just compete, is a necessary skill for success in life.

- Teaching children there is more to the game than winning helps them experience the joy of teamwork.

For Your Heart

Most of us watch in awe as Olympic athletes compete for the gold. The level of competition is unparalleled, and so is the level of respect. The "Golden Rule" of the United States Olympic Committee (USOC) is "real athletes show respect."

Olympians are expected to:

> Congratulate their opponents on their victories, always do what is right, obey the rules of competition, behave on the field in a way that others will admire, and maintain a positive attitude.

Accepting a win with humility, acknowledging a loss with grace, showing respect to the opposing team, and building up teammates who need encouragement is good advice for all of us.

For the Hearts of Your Students

Allow the words of the Olympic Creed to guide your thoughts as you instruct your students:

> The most important thing in the Olympic Games is not to win but to take part, just as the most important thing in life is not the triumph but the struggle. The essential thing is not to have conquered but to have fought well.

Too often in our "it's all about me" society, we teach children how to compete but often neglect to teach them how to cooperate.

In this week's lesson, you have the opportunity to help your students learn *cooperation* and *sportsmanship*. Your students will develop an "Olympic-sized" respect for others—on and off the field.

17 Respecting the Team

COOPERATION—Working with others for everyone's best; choosing to be helpful, not hurtful

SPORTSMANSHIP—Being more concerned with supporting your team than helping yourself

REMEMBER

SKILLS AND OBJECTIVES

- Children will learn that a good sport does not make others feel bad when they lose.
- Children will learn that a good sport does not get upset when he or she loses.
- Children will learn that being a good sport makes the game more fun for everyone.

Turkey Bowl
by Phil Bildner

What does Ethan do to make sure that everyone has fun?

GUIDING CHILDREN'S LEARNING

1. Introduce the definitions for this week's *Heart Attributes*: COOPERATION and SPORTSMANSHIP. Encourage the students to memorize and recite the definitions. They should also listen closely to the story for examples of both *Heart Attributes*.

2. Let's Listen! Read aloud or play the recording of **Bragging and Blaming**

3. After the story, lead your students in the following discussion questions:
   - *Terrell begins bragging about winning the game. What does Tommy do?*
   Tommy stays quiet, and decides not to brag.
   - *Why doesn't Tommy brag? What lesson did he learn in his past?*
   When Tommy played on the Berryville team, he bragged and blamed and he didn't get to be the star of the game as he had hoped. Even though his team won, his attitude probably hurt his relationship with his team. He learned the hard way not to brag anymore.
   - *What does it mean to be a good sport? What kinds of sports are Tommy and Terrell? How can you tell?*
   I know Tommy learned to be a good sport because he used to be a bad sport and learned from his mistakes. He didn't brag or get upset during the game. I know Terrell was not a good sport because he was bragging before the game, and blaming others during the game.
   - *How do you think the story ends? Be creative and come up with your own ending!*

MANNERS IN ACTION

1. At the end of the discussion, point out the **Happle Tree** and how the number of **Happles** is growing. Remind your students that their hearts are growing as well!

2. Here are the *Big Ideas* for discussion this week:
   - A good sport does not make others feel bad when they lose.
   - A good sport does not get upset when he or she loses.
   - A good sport makes the game more fun for everyone.

3. Ask your children how they can show COOPERATION and SPORTSMANSHIP this week. There are opportunities all around us to cooperate with others. Ask the children to name the places and situations that give them an opportunity to be a good sport. Whether on or off the field, respecting the team is something we do every day. Have the children name specific actions that display these Heart Attributes.

Day 1

BRAGGING AND BLAMING

Once upon a heart in Merryville, critters and town folk alike geared up for the biggest soccer game of the year! The showdown between the Merryville Mariners and the Berryville Bears was set to take place in Barringer Park.

Wesley, Jerome, Tommy, Terrell and the rest of the Merryville Mariners were warming up.

"No way they're going to beat us," Wesley said. "We're the fastest team around. I can run circles around their best player."

"Yeah," added Terrell. "They can't stop us, cause they're not as smart as we are."

"Huh, we could beat them with our eyes closed," Jerome laughed. "I'm going to show everybody how good I am today!"

Tommy didn't say much. He knew better. He had learned the hard way when he lived in Berryville that bragging before a game usually got you in trouble!

Before Tommy moved to Merryville, his family lived in Berryville on the other side of Merryville Mountain. He could run faster than any other kid on his team or any other team. Everybody told him he was the best.

Before long, Tommy started bragging about how good he was to his teammates. He never passed the ball. He always took the shot himself.

Before the biggest game of the year, he told everybody in Berryville he was going to make sure his team won. He even said it was a good thing his team had him for a player, because they couldn't win without him.

During the first play of the game, Tommy hogged the ball and charged all the way down the field. One of his teammates was wide open, but he took the shot anyway and missed!

Tommy stomped his feet and said his shoes didn't fit right.

In a few minutes, Tommy ran over a player on the other team and got a penalty flag. He stomped his feet and said the other player ran into him.

Tommy had kept his team from scoring a single point! His teammates complained to the coach during half time.

"Tommy," said Berryville's Coach Cotter. "The best player on a team plays for the team, not for himself. You've been bragging and blaming. That doesn't work on this team. We respect each other and the other team. You'll have to sit out and see what your teammates can do without you."

Tommy was both sad and mad. He didn't like sitting on the bench. He didn't like his teammates complaining about him.

Guess what happened? His teammates scored a goal on the first play of the second half. And they scored again and again, tying the score at 3-3.

Near the end, Coach Cotter finally put Tommy back in the game. Tommy used some fancy footwork to get the ball and barrel down the field. The players on the other team were all over him, staying between Tommy and the goal. Just as he neared the goal, he looked over and saw one of his teammates wide open. He passed the ball. His teammate made an easy score and the buzzer buzzed.

Tommy's team won 4-3! Tommy ran over and congratulated his teammate who had scored the winning goal. His teammate thanked him for a good pass. Together, the whole team celebrated the victory!

It was not long after that day that Tommy's family moved to Merryville. Today, as Tommy was warming up to play and listening to his fellow Mariners brag, he was thinking about the lessons he had learned about bragging and blaming.

The game started and sure enough, Wesley got the ball and ran circles around the Berryville players, but it didn't help his team. He was penalized for illegal moves.

Terrell laughed and said he could handle it. During the next play, the referee heard Terrell tell one of the Berryville players he wasn't smart enough to score. The referee threw Terrell out of the game for taunting! Terrell shouted and pouted as he blamed the other player for taunting him. Terrell was so busy trying to show off, he missed two goals because he was looking around at the crowd to see if they were watching him!

At half time, Merryville's Coach Brooks called his team together and said, "We've forgotten we're a team that doesn't brag or blame. Win or lose, we play with respect!"

Half time ended. All the players came back on the field to play the second half.

A Finish Me Story: What do you think happened next?

17 Respecting the Team

Day 2   ART OF THE HEART®

1. This week, students will be looking for others who are being a good sport. When they find someone, they will give them the **Badge of Honor** that they have made.

2. Instructions:
    - Color the pointed circle blue, the "Badge" circle yellow, and the strips blue.
    - Cut out the circles and strips.
    - Glue the yellow circle to the center of the blue circle.
    - Cut two points into the bottom of the blue strips.
    - Glue the two "ribbons" in place on the back of the badge.

3. Close by reminding students that a good sport is someone who wins well and loses well. Encourage them to be on the lookout to catch someone using good SPORTSMANSHIP!

You'll Need:
- **Badge of Honor** activity sheet (1/student)
- Glue or tape
- Crayons or colored pencils
- Scissors

Day 3   WRITING FROM THE HEART

Ask your students to consider the following journal prompt and answer it according to your classroom writing requirements:

Are you usually a good sport or a bad sport? Explain.

You'll Need:
- **Respecting the Team** activity sheet (1/student)

Days 2-5

Day 4 CREATIVE CONNECTION

You'll Need:
- Whiteboard
- Markers

1. Draw two big circles on the board. Write "Good Sport" in the center of one circle and "Bad Sport" in the other.
2. Begin by reminding students that being part of a team means: working cooperatively, playing by the rules, playing fairly, accepting responsibility for their actions, and having a positive attitude toward others.
3. Pair your students into teams. After each question, give them a little time to consult with each other and give an answer. Write the descriptors in the circles on the board.
4. What does a "Good Sport" look like?
   (Here are some sample descriptors)
   - No name calling.
   - No bad language or curse words.
   - You encourage your teammates.
   - You don't get mad when you lose a game.
   - Use your words to encourage teammates.
   - High-five the other team, win or lose.
   - Follow the rules and don't cheat.
   - Admit when you've made a mistake.

   What does a "Bad Sport" look like?
   (Here are some sample descriptors)
   - You only care about winning.
   - You are angry when you lose.
   - You leave the field or court without congratulating the other team.
   - You "hog the ball" or don't share plays.
   - You criticize your teammates.
   - You don't work together as a team.
   - You think you know better than the coach.
   - You say ugly things to the other team.

5. Ask your students which teammate they would rather be, the "Good Sport" or the "Bad Sport"?

Day 5 TECH TIME

Interactive Whiteboard Activity on MyManners Portal

Can you solve the sport's scramble?!

MANNERS IN ACTION

Whooooo will hang the **Happle** this week?

COOPERATION—Working with others for everyone's best; choosing to be helpful, not hurtful

SPORTSMANSHIP— Being more concerned with supporting your team than helping yourself

WEEK 18
RESPECTING DIFFERENCES

Big Ideas

• Understanding differences as the qualities that make each of us unique opens children's hearts to accept others for who they are.

• Offering acceptance helps others forget their differences.

• We may look or act different on the outside, but we all have the same heart needs on the inside.

For Your Heart

Throughout my grade school years, my mother taught a Sunday School class for adults with limited abilities. One of her students, Carol, sat with us during the worship service that followed the class. Carol liked sitting next to me, so my mother taught me to reach over and squeeze Carol's hand when she became anxious and fidgety, which was a common occurrence.

One particular Sunday, I was the one having trouble sitting still in the pew. Unexpectedly, Carol reached out and squeezed *my* hand. When I looked at her, she winked and nodded as if to communicate she knew how hard it was to stay quiet and sit still through an entire service. Carol's actions taught me a powerful life lesson: On the inside, we're much more alike than different, no matter how much we may differ on the outside!

In everyday living, it is often hard to remember this lesson and even harder to genuinely appreciate the differences. However, it is the acceptance and willingness to learn from our differences that nurtures healthy emotional growth in our families, classrooms, and communities.

For the Hearts of Your Students

When you were a child and someone passed by who looked different from you, didn't your mother always say—"Don't stare!" So, you looked the other way. "Don't stare" soon became "Don't look." Before long, "Don't look" became "Don't see."

In these lessons, you can open the eyes and hearts of your students to the *understanding* that our differences shouldn't be ignored or overlooked, but accepted. Being taught to treat others with respect develops *acceptance* of the unique qualities within each of us. This opens the door to mutual understanding.

You can change the world of tomorrow by instilling acceptance in the hearts of your students today. Their generation can rebuild our society based in mutual respect and understanding.

18 Respecting Differences

UNDERSTANDING—Looking at others and listening to others without judgment

ACCEPTANCE—Treating everyone you meet with the same respect, regardless of differences

REMEMBER

SKILLS AND OBJECTIVES

- Children will learn that people can come from many different cultures and backgrounds.
- Children will learn that we need to show respect for different cultures and ethnicities.

Wise Ol' Wilbur's Recommended Reading

Thank You, Mr. Falker
by Patricia Polacco

How different would Tricia's life have been if she had not had Mr. Falker as her teacher and friend?

GUIDING CHILDREN'S LEARNING

1. Introduce the definitions for this week's *Heart Attributes*: ACCEPTANCE and UNDERSTANDING. Encourage the students to memorize and recite the definitions. They should also listen closely to the story for examples of both *Heart Attributes*.

2. Let's Listen! Read aloud or play the recording of *More Alike Than Different*

3. After the story, lead your students in the following discussion questions:
   - *We know Cap'n Nick lives in the lighthouse and watches for storms. What does Ranger Mick do?*
   Ranger Mick stays in an outpost and watches for forest fires.
   - *What is Heritage Day?*
   It is a day that Merryville celebrates its history and people.
   - *What were the people of Merryville arguing about?*
   How to celebrate Heritage Day.
   - *What do these two friends teach Merryville by their friendship?*
   They teach them not to argue over the differences, but to appreciate them instead. Nick and Mick show their town how to get along even if they don't agree on everything.
   - *Do you have friends from other cultures and backgrounds? What do you appreciate about them?* (Answers will vary)

MANNERS IN ACTION

1. At the end of the discussion, point out the **Happle Tree** and how the number of **Happles** is growing. Remind your students that their hearts are growing as well!

2. Discuss these *Big Ideas*:
   - *People come from many cultures and backgrounds.*
   - *We are more alike than we are different.*
   - *Regardless of differences, we must respect all people.*

3. Ask your children how they can show ACCEPTANCE and UNDERSTANDING this week. When we seek to understand others, we grow in our ACCEPTANCE of them. Have the students identify very specific words and actions they can focus on this week to bring about better relationships everywhere they go.

Day 1

MORE ALIKE THAN DIFFERENT

Once upon a heart in Merryville, there were two best friends, who couldn't be more different...Ranger Mick and Cap'n Nick.

Ranger Mick grew up in a great big log cabin in the Merryville Mountains with lots of brothers and sisters. Cap'n Nick didn't grow up in a house at all. He was raised on a ship at sea without any family.

Ranger Mick spends his days in a lookout post in the mountains. He watches for forest fires and folks in trouble. Ranger Mick's good friends are moose, deer and bears.

Cap'n Nick spends his days in a lighthouse on the shore. He watches for storms and threats from the sea. Cap'n Nick's good friends are cats, dogs and seagulls.

Ranger Mick and Cap'n Nick cheer for different teams, too! Ranger Mick's favorite is the Berryville Bears. Cap'n Nick's favorite is the Merryville Mariners.

They found out they weren't so different after all when they shared a meal at Ranger Mick's house one night. They found out they agreed on the really important things. Didn't take long for them to become best friends! Good thing, 'cause today, they're going to have to teach some folks in Merryville what they learned...that we're a lot more alike on the inside than we are different on the outside.

Folks all over Merryville were fussing about how to celebrate the town's first Heritage Day! Heritage Day was supposed to be a celebration of Merryville's history and people, a time when everyone came together to celebrate how they had grown as a community. The problem was that everybody wanted something different. Nobody could agree on anything. Instead of coming together, they were bickering and arguing, fussing and fighting.

Ranger Mick heard all the commotion from his outpost. Cap'n Nick heard all the commotion from the lighthouse and called his good friend.

"Mick," Cap'n Nick said. "We've got to do something for the folks in town. They're trying so hard to remember where they came from, they've forgotten who they are."

So, Cap'n Nick and Ranger Mick made a plan. They each sounded the alarm from the lighthouse and the outpost. Folks in Merryville stopped their fussing and ran to the town square where picnic tables for Heritage Day were already set for a fine meal.

"Find a seat next to your neighbor," Cap'n Nick said.

"You must be hungry after all the fussing," Ranger Mick added. "Nick and I learned a long time ago the way to settle your differences is to break bread together at the dinner table."

"Bless our food..." Cap'n Nick began. Everyone joined in and then, started eating.

Beans and chicken and salad and bread were passed around the tables. As folks started eating, they started talking, instead of fussing.

"Ahem," Cap'n Nick said, clearing his throat. "Ahem," Ranger Mick followed, clearing his throat. "We have something to share that might just help. Listen to this...

Doesn't matter if you're short or tall, big or small.
Doesn't matter the color of your skin or your next of kin.
Doesn't matter if you live on a boat or a house that can't float.
Doesn't matter if you ride on a tractor or work as an actor.
Doesn't matter if you punch a clock or work on a dock.
Doesn't matter how different we are on the outside,
'Cause we're all the same on the inside.

We need to love and be loved.
We need to hear and be heard.
We need to forgive and be forgiven.
We need to respect and be respected.
We may be different on the outside,
But our hearts are all the same on the inside.
We need to love our neighbors and love this town.
We're more alike than different, so let's calm down."

18 Respecting Differences

Folks nodded their heads in agreement. They shook hands. They hugged. Everyone agreed to work together, instead of working apart. As it all turned out, Heritage Day was the best celebration Merryville ever had!

Just the beginning...

Day 2 ART OF THE HEART®

1. Distribute the **Countries of the World** activity sheets.
2. After your children find the countries of the world, ask them if they can locate any of them on the globe.

You'll Need:
- **Countries of the World** activity sheet (1/student)
- Pencils
- Globe

Day 3 WRITING FROM THE HEART

Ask your students to consider the following journal prompt and answer it according to your classroom writing requirements:

If you could visit any country in the world, which one would you choose to visit? Why?

You'll Need:
- **Respecting Differences** activity sheet (1/student)

Days 2-5

Day 4 CREATIVE CONNECTION

1. Gather your students together and ask them to share their Journal entries from Day 3.

2. As the students share which country they would like to visit, encourage discussion with some of the following questions:
   - *Who would you take with you on your trip to _____ ?*
   - *Do you know anyone who is from there?*
   - *Do you know anyone who has visited there?*
   - *What types of foods or customs do you think may be different in that country?*
   - *Do you think the people look the same as you do or different?*
   - *How do you think the people may be different from you?*
   - *How do you think they may be the same?*

3. People all over the world have much more in common than they do that is different.
   - Everyone smiles when they are happy.
   - Everyone wants to be loved and accepted.
   - Everyone want to have friends.

4. When we meet people from different cultures or countries, we should always remember things about us that are the same and not focus on the things that are different.

You'll Need:
- Journal entries from Day 3
- Globe

Day 5 TECH TIME

Interactive Whiteboard Activity on MyManners Portal

Hello from all the children of the world! Practice your foreign language skills this week!

MANNERS IN ACTION

Whooooo will hang the **Happle** this week?

UNDERSTANDING—Looking at others and listening to others without judgment
ACCEPTANCE—Treating everyone you meet with the same respect, regardless of differences

WEEK 19
RESPECTING PRIVACY

Big Ideas

- Learning to respect the private space and personal belongings of others—especially when no one is looking—helps children develop a deep sense of right and wrong.

- Children learn to share information about others for the right reasons when they learn the difference between tattling and telling.

- Children learn to choose their words carefully when they understand that gossip hurts everyone—the one who is talked about and the one who is doing the talking.

For Your Heart

The concept of privacy has changed drastically in recent years. With Instagram, Snapchat, phone cameras, and reality television, privacy has become an obscure notion. Photos are snapped everywhere at anytime. The most intimate details of people's lives are reported on our newsfeed. Long gone are the days of hiding a diary under your bed for fear of someone learning your innermost thoughts.

We live in a see-all, tell-all, share-all world. And yet, we know as adults, there are some things that should be kept private for protection from humiliation and hurt.

It has been said, "You can tell more about a person by what he says about others than you can by what others say about him." In addition to our words, our actions can reveal the same attitude. Being respectful of the personal space and belongings of others shows the world a great deal about who we are.

For the Hearts of Your Students

Learning to respect privacy is a critically important lesson that reinforces the principle of giving respect and earning respect. With each decision to consider the feelings of someone else before making a decision to breach their privacy, children develop a safeguard for their behavior.

In this week's lesson, you'll help your students learn the importance of respecting privacy as an essential component of getting along with others. Teaching them to be *considerate* of the feelings of others, establishes the foundation for integrity in their lives. Children who understand this concept and put it into action become *trustworthy* and earn the respect of their teachers and peers.

19 Respecting Privacy

CONSIDERATE—Taking into account the feelings of others before you speak or act

TRUSTWORTHY—Doing what you said you would do when you said you would do it

REMEMBER

SKILLS AND OBJECTIVES

- Children will learn what gossiping is and why it is hurtful to others.
- Children will learn what to do if friends are gossiping.
- Children will learn why it is important to keep a friend's secret.

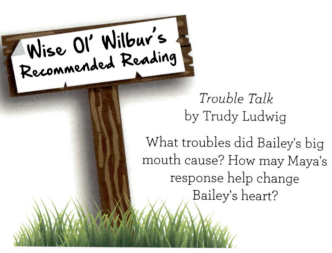

Trouble Talk
by Trudy Ludwig

What troubles did Bailey's big mouth cause? How may Maya's response help change Bailey's heart?

GUIDING CHILDREN'S LEARNING

1. Introduce the definitions for this week's *Heart Attributes*: CONSIDERATE and TRUSTWORTHY. Encourage the students to memorize and recite the definitions. They should also listen closely to the story for examples of both *Heart Attributes*.

2. Let's Listen! Read aloud or play the recording of ***Who Said, You Said***

3. After the story, lead your students in the following discussion questions:
   - *Respecting privacy means respecting the space and stuff of others, but there is another way to respect someone's privacy- don't gossip! Who was hurt by the spread of gossip in the story?*
   Mary's Granny
   - *What happened when Carolina the Cow spread the first piece of gossip?*
   It changed and was not what was originally said.
   - *What happened over and over again in the story?*
   The message changed every time someone shared it!
   - *What happens when we gossip?*
   Sometimes others are hurt by what is said and what we say is not usually accurate.
   - *What could have happened in the story to Granny's and Mrs. McDonald's friendship?*
   It could have been damaged by gossip that was spread by others.

MANNERS IN ACTION

1. At the end of the discussion, look at the definitions of the *Heart Attributes* and remind your students that their hearts are growing in many ways this year.

2. Discuss these *Big Ideas* with your students:
   - *Gossiping is hurtful to others*
   - *We should not gossip or encourage others to gossip.*
   - *It is important to keep our friends' secrets.*

3. Ask your children how they can be CONSIDERATE and TRUSTWORTHY this week. What are situations at school and at home where they can grow in these *Heart Attributes*? What do they plan to do differently this week than they have done in the past? By the end of the week, ask the students to share their stories with the rest of the class and hang the Happles on the Happle Tree.

Day 1

WHO SAID, YOU SAID

Once upon a heart in Merryville, Wise Ol' Wilbur was sitting on the kitchen window sill visiting with Mrs. McDonald while she was baking pies. Nobody in Merryville loves the smell of happle pies more than Wilbur. Soon, Mary came by to pick up a fresh pie for her Granny.

"Good Morning, Wilbur," Mary said as she stepped on the porch to Mrs. McDonald's house.

"It's a good morning, indeed," answered Wilbur.

"Good Morning, Mary," said Mrs. McDonald. "I have a happle pie ready for your Granny. I added a little of my special extra goodness for her. I know how much she loves my pies."

"She sure does, Mrs. McDonald," said Mary. "She's always telling everybody how great your pies are!"

Mrs. McDonald chuckled. "Mary, be sure and tell your Granny, I think she's great!"

"I'll do it," answered Mary. "Have a good day baking!"

"Bye, Wilbur. You have a good day, too!" Mary said, heading back to her Granny's.

Carolina the Cow was munching grass in the pasture near the porch and overheard what Mrs. McDonald said. Carolina walked over to Helen the Horse and said, "I can't believe Mrs. McDonald thinks that Mary's granny is always late!"

"Well, that's not a nice thing to say, but maybe she's right," thought Helen.

Since it was a very hot day in Merryville, Helen clopped down to the pond to get a cool drink. Gracie the Goose was there enjoying an afternoon swim.

"Gracie," said Helen, "Did you know that Mary's granny broke Mrs. McDonald's pie plate?"

"Do tell," honked Gracie. "Why in the world would Granny break Mrs. McDonald's pie plate?" Then Gracie swam to the other side of the pond.

Freddie the Frog was sunning on his lily pad when Gracie swam by. "Freddie, did you know that Mrs. McDonald broke Granny's garden gate?"

"Oh, no!" croaked Freddie. "Granny loved her garden gate." Freddie stretched back on his pad to catch a few more sun rays, but he couldn't stop thinking about how upset Granny must be about her broken garden gate. Penelope the raccoon was sitting on an old log near the edge of the pond. She had just finished eating a snack, so she was washing her hands, as raccoons always do.

"Hey, Freddie," said Penelope. "What are you up to today?"

"Penelope, I'm worried about Mary's granny," answered Freddie.

"Why, what happened?" asked Penelope.

"You didn't hear?" replied Freddie. "Mrs. McDonald said Mary's granny is so overweight, she can't get through her garden gate!"

Penelope couldn't believe Mrs. McDonald would say such a nasty thing about Mary's granny. "Why that doesn't sound like something Mrs. McDonald would ever say," thought Penelope. Penelope was so upset, she ran to find her brother, Peter, to ask him what to do. She found him resting in his favorite tree outside Granny's kitchen window.

"Peter," called Penelope. "I'm so upset I don't know what to do. Mrs. McDonald is telling people all over Merryville that Granny is so overweight, she can't get through her garden gate." Penelope didn't notice that Granny's kitchen window was open. Granny stuck her head out the window and hollered, "What did you say, Penelope?" just as Mary walked through the kitchen door with Mrs. McDonald's fresh happle pie in her hand.

"Well, why I never," exclaimed Granny as she grabbed the happle pie from Mary and stormed out the door for Mrs. McDonald's house. She was really, really mad that Mrs. McDonald would say such an awful thing about her. Mary tried to stop her, but couldn't. Mary thought she knew what had happened, so she went straight to Penelope.

"Penelope, who told you what Mrs. McDonald said?" asked Mary.

"It was Freddie the Frog," answered Penelope.

Mary went straight to Freddie the Frog.

"Freddie, who told you what Mrs. McDonald said?"

"It was Gracie the Goose," answered Freddie.

Mary went straight to Gracie the Goose.

"Gracie, who told you what Mrs. McDonald said?"

"It was Helen the Horse," honked Gracie.

Mary went straight to Helen the Horse.

"Helen, who told you what Mrs. McDonald said?"

19 Respecting Privacy

"It was Carolina the Cow," answered Helen.

Mary went straight to Carolina the Cow.

"Carolina, who told you what Mrs. McDonald said?"

Carolina replied, "I heard it with my own two ears as I was munching grass."

Meanwhile, Granny passed a lot of folks on the way to Mrs. McDonald's. She thought everybody was looking at her like she was big as a house. By the time she got to Mrs. McDonald's, she wasn't nearly as mad as she was sad.

Mrs. McDonald saw Granny coming with the pie, so she ran to the porch to greet her dear friend, not knowing she was mad and sad. "Is something wrong with the pie?" asked Mrs. McDonald.

"How could I eat THIS pie, after what you said?" snapped Granny.

Mary ran up. "Wait! Wait! I can set the record straight," she said to the two upset ladies.

"Mrs. McDonald, Freddie said you said, 'Granny's so overweight she can't get through her garden gate.'"

"And Gracie said you said, 'Mrs. McDonald broke Granny's garden gate.'"

"And Helen said you said, 'Granny broke Mrs. McDonald's pie plate.'"

"And Carolina said you said, 'Granny's always late.'"

"But what you really said was that you think Granny's great!'"

"Oh, Mrs. McDonald," Granny said, hugging her dear friend. "I knew you wouldn't say that awful thing about me, even if I do eat too many of your happle pies!"

"Seems to me, there's too much gossip in Merryville these days," Mrs. McDonald said, shaking her head. "Let's go in and have a cup of tea and a slice of pie."

"Yes, indeed," Granny agreed.

Just the beginning...

Day 2   ART OF THE HEART®

1. Pass out the **No Gossip Allowed** activity sheets and ask students to take a few moments to fill them out quietly.

2. When the class is finished, discuss the following answers with them:
    - Gossip is <u>talking</u> about someone else.
    - Gossip is saying things about <u>someone</u> else that aren't nice.
    - Gossip may or may not be <u>true</u>.
    - Gossip can ruin <u>friendships</u>.
    - If someone gossips, ask them how they would <u>feel</u> if someone said something unkind about them.
    - <u>Walk</u> away if they do not stop spreading gossip.
    - Never repeat gossip that you <u>hear</u>.

3. Continue the discussion on Day 4.

You'll Need:
- No Gossip Allowed! activity sheet
- Pencils

Day 3   WRITING FROM THE HEART

Ask your students to consider the following journal prompt and answer it according to your classroom writing requirements:

Why do you think gossip hurts friendships?

You'll Need:
- Respecting Privacy activity sheet (1/student)

Days 2-5

Day 4 CREATIVE CONNECTION

1. Ask your students to summarize what they have learned over the last few days about gossip.

2. Remind them:
    - Friends are people you trust and depend on.
    - Private information shared with a friend should not be shared with anyone else.
    - When you hear others spreading gossip, remind them of the Golden Rule.
    - Walk away if they continue to gossip.
    - It is important to tell an adult something you hear if you think someone is in danger.

3. Have your students sit in a circle to play the Telephone Game. Start the game with a full sentence and then have the students whisper it to their neighbor. By the time it reaches the end, the sentence is usually nothing like the original. This is how gossips spreads and warps as it is passed around.

4. Ask your students to draw the comparisons between the Telephone Game and gossip.

You'll Need:
- **No Gossip Allowed** activity sheets from Day 2
- **Journal Answers** from Day 3

Day 5 TECH TIME

Interactive Whiteboard Activity on MyManners Portal

Carolina Cow has a secret! Watch what happens when news gets passed around.

MANNERS IN ACTION

Whoooooo will hang the **Happle** this week?

CONSIDERATE—Taking into account the feelings of others before you speak or act
TRUSTWORTHY—Doing what you said you would do when you said you would do it

WEEK 20
RESPECTING PROPERTY

Big Ideas

- Respecting others' belongings shows appreciation for the person to whom it belongs.

- Taking responsibility to put things back and care for them properly helps children develop maturity and integrity.

- Children develop honesty by learning to appreciate and respect the work and ideas of others as personal property.

For Your Heart

If you've ever spent time around a toddler, you probably know they have a special set of rules when it comes to property:

- If I like it, it's mine.
- If it's in my hand, it's mine.
- If I can take it from you, it's mine.
- If I had it a little while ago, it's still mine.
- If it looks just like mine, it's mine.
- If I saw it first, it's mine.
- If I'm doing or building something, all the pieces are mine.
- If it's broken, it's yours.

These are true, aren't they? Unfortunately, in today's world these rules extend well beyond the preschool classroom!

For the Hearts of Your Students

How can you help your elementary age children move beyond the toddler rules? Offer them a new set of rules with a new point of view.

In this week's lesson, you'll help your students understand the importance of respecting property – whether it is their own or someone else's. Your students will gain *appreciation* for the generosity of their classmates as they learn the give-and-take of sharing. You'll find great satisfaction in watching your students begin taking *responsibility* in how they care for their own possessions, the belongings of others and school property.

20 Respecting Property

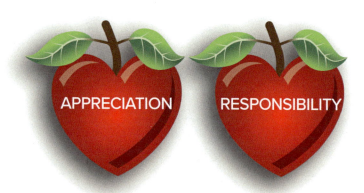

APPRECIATION—Recognizing and acknowledging value in people, places and things

RESPONSIBILITY—Following through on your duties without supervision

REMEMBER

SKILLS AND OBJECTIVES

- Children will gain an understanding of property.
- Children will learn why it is important to respect the belongings of others.
- Children will consider cheating as stealing someone else's property.

Mandy
by Julie Edwards

How might this story have ended if Mandy had not cared for the deserted cottage?

GUIDING CHILDREN'S LEARNING

1. Introduce the definitions for this week's *Heart Attributes*: APPRECIATION and RESPONSIBILITY. Encourage your students to memorize and recite the definitions. They should also listen closely to the story for examples of both *Heart Attributes*.

2. Let's Listen! Read aloud or play the recording of ***Tommy Tripper's Trouble***

3. After the story, lead your students in the following discussion questions:
   - *Do you think Tommy intended to cause so much trouble for everyone?*
     No! He was just careless.
   - *What do you think was the main cause for Tommy's mishaps?*
     He was in a hurry and didn't realize he had left the barn door and the gate open. He didn't even realize he had spilled the paint!
   - *One mishap can lead to a string of mishaps! What happened to the Mayor of Merryville?*
     He had blue gooseprints all over his new suit.
   - *What did you think of Tommy's attitude at the end of the story?*
     He was sorry for being careless, apologized and then began cleaning up the messes.
   - *Do you sometimes forget to follow the words of Cap'n Nick? Share some of your stories!*

MANNERS IN ACTION

1. At the end of the discussion, look at the definitions of the *Heart Attributes* and remind your students that showing RESPONSIBILITY with someone else's property, shows APPRECIATION for them.

2. Discuss these *Big Ideas* with your students:
   - *It is important to be very careful with things that are borrowed from someone else.*
   - *Property can be things both seen and unseen.*
   - *Copying someone else's work is a way of stealing another's property.*

3. Ask your children how they can show APPRECIATION and RESPONSIBILITY this week. Showing RESPONSIBILITY for their property and the property of others shows great APPRECIATION for all they have. What can they do this week to show a new understanding of Respecting Property? Ask the students to spot instances they see others demonstrating these *Heart Attributes*.

Day 1

TOMMY TRIPPER'S TROUBLE

Once upon a heart in Merryville, kids gathered at the lighthouse to listen to Cap'n Nick tell one of his famous stories. Today, he was telling about the day Tommy Tripper forgot an important lesson and everything went wrong in Merryville. So Cap'n Nick began...

Tommy Tripper's dad was trying to fix up some things at the Trout Farm, but he needed a special wrench that he didn't own. He knew Ol' McDonald probably had the tool in his barn, so he sent Tommy over to fetch it.

"Tommy, be sure and ask Mrs. McDonald if you can borrow a wrench from the barn. I'm sure she won't mind, but don't forget to ask."

"Sure thing, Dad. I'll be back before you know it," answered Tommy as he sped off on his bike.

In a flash he was at Mrs. McDonald's door. He knocked twice and opened the door as he called out her name, "Mrs. McDonald, it's Tommy. My dad needs to borrow a wrench from the barn."

"Come on in, Tommy. That's fine with me. Go on out to the barn and get what you need," said Mrs. McDonald. "You can grab a cookie on your way out." Tommy grabbed a fresh warm cookie as he raced out the back door to the barn.

The barn door was closed, but Tommy knew how to slide it open. Inside was every tool anyone could ever need. Tommy looked around awhile trying to find the one his dad needed. He finally saw it, but it was out of reach. He grabbed a paint can to stand on, so he could reach the wrench. He ran out the barn door as fast he could, because he knew his dad was waiting.

Tommy was in such a hurry he didn't notice the paint can turned over when he jumped down from the table, spilling bright blue paint all over the barn floor.

Tommy ran across the yard and hollered, "Thanks, Mrs. McDonald for the wrench and the cookie," as he unlocked the side gate and jumped on his bike to speed back to Tripper's Trout Farm.

Now, this is when the trouble started, added Cap'n Nick, because you see...

Tommy went in the front door, but didn't close it behind him. He ran out the back door and left it wide open. Tommy slid the barn door to the side, but didn't slide it back. When he jumped on his bike, he left the side gate open, too!

In a blink, Sketch the Skunk went in the front door. KC the kitty cat went in the back door. Gracie the Goose went in the barn. And, Carolina the Cow meandered out the side yard and trotted down the street.

Sketch the Skunk was sniffing around when Mrs. McDonald found him and screamed. When she screamed, Sketch got scared. And when skunks get scared, they spew stinky stuff everywhere. It was awful!!!!! Mrs. McDonald wondered how in the world Sketch got into her house.

Just then, Mrs. McDonald heard a crash in the back of the house. She ran into the kitchen to find KC licking up spilled milk from a broken glass on the floor. "KC, what have you done? How did you get in my kitchen?" asked a very upset Mrs. McDonald. She clapped her hands and shooed him out the back door.

When she looked up, she saw Gracie the Goose waddling out of the barn. She became even more upset when she saw the big blue gooseprints Gracie was leaving behind. She ran to the barn and found a puddle of bright blue paint. Before she could grab Gracie, Gracie was waddling through the open side gate for downtown.

Then, Mrs. McDonald turned and realized Carolina the Cow was not in the side yard. In the distance she heard Carolina mooing a happy moo. "Oh, no," she thought, "I bet Carolina found her way to Miss Charlotte's Chocolate Shoppe. She just loves Miss Charlotte's milk chocolate."

Mrs. McDonald ran out the side gate and down the street. She followed Gracie's gooseprints all the way to the Mayor's office. The Mayor was holding Gracie with a scowl on his face. He had bright blue paint all over his new suit.

"Moooo, Moooo," sang Carolina the Cow from the Chocolate Shoppe. Mrs. McDonald ran across the street with Gracie under her arm to stop Carolina from eating any more milk chocolate.

Mrs. McDonald apologized to the Mayor and Miss Charlotte for all the mess Gracie and Carolina had made. Just then, Tommy Tripper came down the street on his way to Miss Charlotte's. His dad had given him a quarter for his help, and he was going to spend it in the Chocolate Shoppe.

When Mrs. McDonald saw Tommy, she realized all the trouble started after he had been at her house that morning. "Tommy, did you close the front door after you opened it this morning?" asked Mrs. McDonald.

Tommy said, "Uh, No, Ma'am. I guess not," in a quiet voice. "And Tommy, did you close the back door when you went out to the barn?" Again, Tommy said, "Uh, No, Ma'am. I guess not," in a quieter voice. "And Tommy, did you close the barn door when you left the barn?" "Uh, No, Ma'am. I guess not," Tommy said in an even quieter voice. "And Tommy, did you lock the side gate when you left the side yard?"

"Uh, No, Ma'am. I guess not," Tommy whispered.

20 Respecting Property

The Mayor chimed in and said, "Tommy, maybe you'll never forget that if you open it, you close it. If you spill it, you clean it up. If you unlock it, you lock it. And if you take it out, you put it back. And, I would suggest when you take back Mrs. McDonald's wrench, you clean up the spilled paint and Gracie's gooseprints all along the way. Is that a deal?"

"Yes Sir," answered Tommy. "I won't let this ever happen again. I promise!"

So, Cap'n Nick turned to the class and said, *"I hope you learned the same lessons from this story that Tommy learned in real life."*

If you open it, close it.
If you turn it on, turn it off.
If you unlock it, lock it.
If you spill it, clean it up.
If you take it out, put it back.
If you break it, fix it.

Just the beginning...

Day 2 MUSIC OF THE HEART®

1. Write **Wilbur's Words of Wisdom** on the board.

   What's yours is yours
   So it's not mine-
   To copy your work
   Would be a crime
   I'll work real hard,
   And in due time
   I'll earn that grade
   With my own mind!

2. Divide students into groups of 4-5.

3. Give the groups a few minutes in separate parts of the room to create a rap with motions.

4. Have each group perform their rap for the class and vote on the best one!

5. Before big tests, have the students rap **Wilbur's Words of Wisdom** as a good reminder to never cheat!

You'll Need:
Wilbur's Words of Wisdom

Day 3 WRITING FROM THE HEART

Ask your students to consider the following journal prompt and answer it according to your classroom writing requirements:

How do you feel when you get a really good grade on a test? Would you feel differently if you had cheated to get that grade?

You'll Need:
- **Respecting Property** activity sheet (1/student)

Days 2-5

Day 4 CREATIVE CONNECTION

1. Ask your students to share some of their thoughts from the Journal Prompt on Day 3.

2. Continue with a discussion using the following questions and comments.
   How does it feel to take credit for something that is not yours?
   How does it feel to have someone else take credit for your work?

3. Close the discussion today by emphasizing the following points.
   - Cheating is when you take answers from someone else or take credit for work that you did not do.
   - When someone puts their name on your work, it is hurtful. When you put your name on someone else's work, you don't feel proud of that accomplishment because you know you did not do the work.
   - Cheating keeps you from exercising your brain and learning.
   - Down the road, cheating can be very serious. For example, kids get kicked out of high school or college for cheating, and adults lose their jobs or even end up in jail, depending on what kind of cheating has been done.

You'll Need:
- Journal Prompt from Day 3

Day 5 TECH TIME

Interactive Whiteboard Activity on MyManners Portal

I repeat, Don't cheat!

MANNERS IN ACTION

Whooooo will hang the **Happle** this week?

APPRECIATION—Recognizing and acknowledging value in people, places and things
RESPONSIBILITY—Following through on your duties without supervision

WEEK 21
RESPECTING YOUR COMMUNITY

Big Ideas

- Civility shows respect for others in your community.
- Communities function more smoothly, efficiently, and pleasantly when both adults and children practice common respect for others.
- Respectful communities count on the reinforcement of respectful behavior in classrooms.

For Your Heart

A well-known and well-respected college football coach thunders "One team! One heartbeat!" to his players at the end of every practice and at the opening of every game. He drives home the belief that winning happens when you're playing for the team, not playing for yourself. His team members understand they represent their university and state, on *and* off the field.

This is a coach who wants to produce men who become good citizens.

In after-game interviews, players emphasize fulfilling their role on the team, not their own personal goals. In a loss, they're quick to take responsibility. In a win, they are quick to share the credit.

This is an excellent example of preparing students to live unselfishly in community for the good of others.

For the Hearts of Your Students

You can infuse the same respect in your students by helping them learn what it means to be part of something bigger than themselves. Emphasizing "one heartbeat" can be the reminder that "we're all in this together"—in the classroom, school and community.

Education is much more than imparting knowledge. *Webster's* 1828 edition defines education as:

> *Education comprehends all that series of instruction and discipline, which is intended to enlighten the understanding, correct the temper, and form the manners and habits of youth, and fit them for usefulness in their future stations.*

In this week's lesson, you can help your students understand the importance of being *civil* in our community and their role in acting respectfully in all situations. You have the honor of teaching your students how to make *appropriate* choices as they grow into their "future stations" of life.

21 Respecting Your Community

CIVIL—To respect others and self for the betterment of community

APPROPRIATE—Knowing the right thing to say or do in any given situation

REMEMBER

SKILLS AND OBJECTIVES

- Children will consider their behavior as a member of their community.
- Children will consider their responsibilities as a member of their community.
- Children will learn why it is important to behave appropriately in public places, such as the mall.

Charlie and the Chocolate Factory by Ronald Doahl

What is your opinion of the children's behavior in the factory? Does it show respect for others?

GUIDING CHILDREN'S LEARNING

1. Begin the lesson by introducing this week's *Heart Attributes*: CIVIL and APPROPRIATE. Review the definitions throughout the week.

2. Let's Listen! Read aloud or play the recording of **The Fountain of Life**

3. After the story, lead your students in the following discussion questions:
   - *Why was Ol' McDonald working on the fountain?*
     It wasn't flowing very smoothly.
   - *Was it Ol' McDonald's job to fix the fountain?*
     It was not his official job. He volunteered to do it because he was being a good citizen and his father had done it before him.
   - *How did Tommy fix the fountain's flow?*
     He climbed to the spring's source and removed a boulder.
   - *Now that Mr. McDonald is old, who will take care of the fountain?*
     Tommy!
   - *Did Florence realize who was keeping the fountain flowing?*
     No- it was a secret between Tommy and Mr. McDonald
   - *What did Tommy show responsibility in this story?*
     He volunteered to climb to the spring's source so that the fountain would continue to flow freely.

MANNERS IN ACTION

1. As citizens of a community, it is our responsibility to show APPROPRIATE and CIVIL behavior. Did Ol' McDonald and Tommy do this?

2. Discuss these *Big Ideas*:
   - As a citizen, I am responsible to help care for my community.
   - As a citizen, I should use CIVIL and APPROPRIATE behavior.
   - It is important to behave in public places, such as the mall.

3. Our behavior in public places reflects our awareness of those around us. Challenge your students to think about their behavior at school, at home, at the mall, park or library. As the class specifically discusses APPROPRIATE behavior in a shopping mall, ask them what rules would apply to any public place. At the end of the week, have them tell stories of awareness of behavior in public places.

Day 1

THE FOUNTAIN OF LIFE

Once upon a heart in Merryville, there was an ancient fountain in the center of town. The oldest memory of the oldest townsperson couldn't reach back to a time when the fountain didn't gurgle and splash joyfully and smooth. Three pools tumbled into each other, the lowest and the largest of which was dotted with lily pads.

You could hear it faintly, at the end of the lane, from the open windows of Charlotte's Chocolate Shoppe. You could see the afternoon sun's glittering refractions on the walls of Armand's bakery. It was even rumored that a natural spring, trickling out of the depths of Merryville Mountain, fed it with fresh water every day.

Tommy had first seen the fountain when his family moved to the trout farm. Ever since then, he felt most at home sitting on its edge, listening to its ripply song and imagining all the town events which had taken place around it. He had heard that Ol' McDonald, resting on one knee, had proposed to Mrs. McDonald by the fountain, that Armand had read all of the letters from his family in Paris on its mossy rim. He had even heard that Florence had nurtured her first flower seeds with cool water drawn from its basin.

This morning, Tommy had decided to walk to school. The sun was barely peeking from around the mountain, the shops weren't even open, and yet Tommy heard the tip-tap of old leather shoes on the cobblestone boulevard. Off in the distance, Ol' McDonald was walking toward the fountain with a toolbox propped on one shoulder.

"Hello, Mr. McDonald," the young boy said, staring into the kind and wrinkly old face of Merryville's oldest citizen.

"Good morning, Tommy!"

Tommy nodded. The old man smiled warmly, placed his toolbox among the blown fall leaves, and took out a long, fuzzy wire. Tommy scrunched his eyebrows inquiringly.

"This is a pipe cleaner," the old man explained.

Tommy was fascinated. Ol' McDonald's hands trembled slightly as he angled the wire into the first tube of the fountain. The water sputtered everywhere. As the cleaner snaked in, bits of gunk and debris filtered out and landed in the fountain. When he was done, the flows from the spouts were fuller and clearer.

"I didn't know this was your job!" Tommy said, a little envious.

"Oh, it's not."

"It's not? Then why do you have to do it?"

"It doesn't have to be my job for it to be my responsibility," said Ol' McDonald slowly. "This town has taken care of me all my life. I do what I can to take care of it."

Several weeks went by, and Tommy noticed that the fountain's spouts sputtered weaker every day. He even went one morning to see if Ol' McDonald was fixing it, but instead, he found the old man sitting on the edge, lightly stroking the water.

"Is it broken?" Tommy blurted out.

"I am not sure. I thought it might have been the pipes, but those are clear."

"Someone will fix it. Right?"

Ol' McDonald chuckled. "Now of that, I am not sure. Many people appreciate the fountain, but few care for it."

"That's not fair."

"Nope," Ol' McDonald smiled again. "But I think I may know what is wrong. The pipes on this end are clear and clean, but I am not as spry as I used to be and I haven't gone to check on the pipes up the mountain."

"So it's true? It comes from the mountain? Let me go! I'm spry!"

Ol' McDonald rested a hand on the young boy's shoulder. "My father took care of this fountain before he passed. If you'd like, I can show you how to care for it, so that it never stops flowing. But not many will ask it of you, and even fewer will thank you."

"I don't need them to thank me," whispered Tommy. "It has been kind to me and that is enough."

"Well, then. Follow the trail at the end of the road. Listen to the babbling of the brook and track it all the way up. It may take you awhile, but soon you will come to where the water flows out of the mountain."

Tommy started up and didn't stop. At times, the trees were so dense that the air looked thick and green. Several times, he tripped and had to pick thorns from his skin and clothes. He strained to hear the whispered babbling. It floated in and out, in and out, of his hearing. His breathing grew heavier, and more than once he turned back toward town. But something propelled him forward.

Finally, he heard it loud and clear. He pushed several branches out of his way and saw what Ol' McDonald had described to him. Two enormous boulders leaned against one another in an ancient and terrifying triangle. At its base,

135

21 Respecting Your Community

from a scraggly hole in the mountain, trickled the silvery liquid.

Immediately, Tommy saw what had gone wrong. A giant rock had wedged itself in the opening of the spring. The water could barely escape. Determined, Tommy rolled up his sleeves.

Aaaagggghhhh, he grunted loudly. He was gasping. The rock barely budged. Again and again he put his strength against the rock, but it won out. *Is this even worth it?* Suddenly, an idea came to him. He had seen Ol' McDonald do something similar when he was repairing his home after a storm and there were fallen logs around.

Tommy found the straightest, strongest branch he could find. Then, he found a smaller, movable rock. He squirmed the branch under the boulder, placed it on top of the smaller rock and pushed as hard as he could down to the ground. The lever and fulcrum worked! With a *whoosh* and a rumble, the boulder jiggled, lifted and tumbled down the slope. Water gushed out like it had never seen the light of day. Tommy leaned back and wiped the sweat from his forehead, satisfied.

When he got back into town, the fountain was splashing merrily. Ol' McDonald was beaming from ear to ear and Florence was drawing water.

"This old thing just keeps trickling away. I do imagine it'll trickle that way long after I'm gone," Florence half-said, half-sung.

Ol' McDonald caught the eyes of the boy with his own. He winked.

Just the beginning...

Day 2   ART OF THE HEART®

Prep: Cut **JAR** scenarios out and place in jar.

1. Begin by explaining that this week we are talking about respecting our community with CIVIL and APPROPRIATE behavior in public places such as a mall.

2. Introduce the **JAR** and tell students it stands for "Just Act Respectfully". One at a time, pull a scenario out of the **JAR** and ask students to tell you what respectful behavior would be in that scenario. Allow students to take turns acting out the different scenarios when APPROPRIATE.

3. One fun option is to have a right and a wrong answer acted out at the same time.

4. There are 16 scenarios. Choose 8 for Day 2 and the remaining 8 on Day 4.

You'll Need:
- Large jar or container
- **JAR** activity sheet (1/classroom)
- Scissors

Day 3   WRITING FROM THE HEART

Ask your students to consider the following journal prompt and answer it according to your classroom writing requirements:

Have you ever heard someone speaking disrespectfully to someone working in a store or the mall? How do you think it made them feel?

You'll Need:
- *Respecting Your Community* activity sheet (1/student)

Day 4 CREATIVE CONNECTION

1. Continue the **JAR** activity from Day 2 until the class has read and acted out all remaining scenarios from the **JAR**.

2. Remind students that showing CIVIL and APPROPRIATE behavior at the mall helps create a more respectful environment for everyone who is there.

You'll Need:
- **JAR** scenarios from Day 2

Day 5 TECH TIME

Interactive Whiteboard Activity on MyManners Portal

Try to navigate the ins and outs of the mall in this fun game!

MANNERS IN ACTION

Whooooo will hang the **Happle** this week?

CIVIL—To respect others and self for the betterment of community
APPROPRIATE—Knowing the right thing to say or do in any given situation

WEEK 22
RESPECTING OUR COUNTRY

Big Ideas

- When we teach children to appreciate the freedoms of our country, we help them develop respect for those who defend our country.

- Reciting the Pledge of Allegiance teaches children to respect our nation's flag.

- Learning the meaning of the words in the Pledge of Allegiance helps them understand the importance of keeping promises.

For Your Heart

Not long ago, nearly 450 high school seniors filed onto the main floor of a college basketball arena to take their seats for the graduation ceremony. Family members and friends filled the balcony seats. A growing sense of excitement filled the arena. An elderly gentleman in a wheelchair was seated near the stage for an up-close view of his great-grandson's graduation.

The band began to play the National Anthem, but the music could hardly be heard over the chatter of the crowd. Few were looking for the flag, attempting to sing along or standing still with their hands over their hearts. But among these few was the old gentleman. Despite his feebleness, he managed to push himself up from his wheelchair to show respect for his country. His frail body found strength to stand through the power of his patriotism.

For the Hearts of Your Students

Being an American citizen is a great honor. With that honor comes great responsibility. You can be a part of bringing a return of true patriotism to this generation by instilling an appreciation for the freedoms we enjoy in our country in the hearts of your students.

In this week's lesson, you can be a part of inspiring *patriotism* in this generation by helping your students understand and appreciate the privilege of American *citizenship*.

French sociologist Alexis de Tocqueville (1805-1859) traveled to the United States in 1831 to study our prisons, but broadened his study to the meaning of democracy. In his 1835 treatise, "Democracy in America", he noted, "America is great because she is good. If America ceases to be good, America will cease to be great."

You can help this generation ensure America will continue to be great, by encouraging them to be good citizens who never take our freedoms for granted.

22 Respecting Our Country

PATRIOTISM—Loving our country enough to protect it and the principles upon which it was founded

CITIZENSHIP—An attitude of cooperation and social responsibility

REMEMBER

SKILLS AND OBJECTIVES

- Children will learn that many people have fought for our freedom.
- Children will learn how we can show appreciation for the service of soldiers.
- Children will learn what it means to be a good citizen.

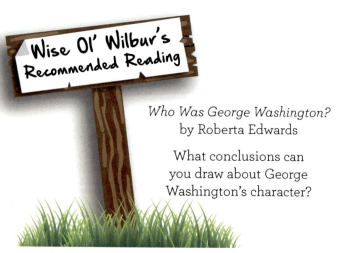

Who Was George Washington? by Roberta Edwards

What conclusions can you draw about George Washington's character?

GUIDING CHILDREN'S LEARNING

1. Begin the lesson by introducing the *Heart Attributes* for the week, CITIZENSHIP and PATRIOTISM.

2. It's Story Time! Read aloud or listen to the recording of **The Little Patriot With the Big Heart**

3. After the story, lead your students in the following discussion:
   - *What does Jack find in the closet that he brings out to Grandpa?*
     A box of medals, ribbons, and photographs.
   - *What can you tell about Jack's relationship with his grandfather?*
     Jack loves his grandpa and respects him a lot, because he wants to spend time with him and listens respectfully to his stories and advice.
   - *What is a PATRIOT?*
     Someone who loves their country and does their part to make it great.
   - *What does Jack do for Sergeant Joe?*
     He helps him stand up to show respect for the flag.
   - *Do you know anyone who has fought in a war for our country? How might you show your PATRIOTISM by respecting this person, or anyone who has fought for our country?*
     By saluting or clapping for someone in uniform.
     By saying "thank you" to someone in uniform.
     By looking for ways to help a soldier or veteran.

MANNERS IN ACTION

1. Review the definitions of the *Heart Attributes*, CITIZENSHIP and PATRIOTISM.

2. Discuss these *Big Ideas* with the students:
   - Many people have fought for our freedom.
   - We should show appreciation for the service of soldiers.
   - CITIZENSHIP and PATRIOTISM show our gratitude for those who have fought for our freedom.

3. How can we demonstrate CITIZENSHIP and PATRIOTISM? Challenge your students to think about the freedoms we have in the United States and how we can show gratitude for the privilege of living here. Showing respect for the flag, the *Pledge of Allegiance*, the *National Anthem* and for our service men and women are ways that we can grow in CITIZENSHIP and PATRIOTISM!

Day 1

THE LITTLE PATRIOT WITH A BIG HEART

Once upon a heart in Merryville, Jack's grandpa lived in one of the great old houses on Walnut Street. Jack loved playing checkers with his grandpa on the big front porch. When Jack lost a game, Grandpa would always say, "Let's go for two out of three." The day they went five out of nine, Grandpa decided it was time to take a break from checkers. He patted Jack on the shoulder and said, "Jack, I want you to go look in my bedroom closet for an old brown shoebox that holds my marble collection. I want to show you the champion marble my grandpa gave me when I was your age."

Jack ran to Grandpa's room and opened the closet door. There were lots of shoeboxes on the floor! He opened the first box. It was filled with letters. He wondered if they were love letters from Grandma to Grandpa. The next box Jack opened was full of old fishing baits. He set it aside for later, so he could ask Grandpa about going fishing.

Then Jack saw a brown shoebox taped together, sitting in the back corner of the closet. It looked as old as Grandpa. *That's gotta' be it*, Jack thought, as he struggled to pull off the tape holding the box together. But when he looked inside, there were no marbles to be found, only bright colored ribbons and medals with photographs of soldiers. He picked up the box and ran back to the porch with a hundred questions for Grandpa.

"Grandpa, Grandpa," shouted Jack. "Look what I found!" Grandpa chuckled and said, "Let's see what ya' got." When Grandpa saw the box, the excitement in his voice turned to sadness, and so did his face. "What's wrong, Grandpa?" asked Jack. "Jack, that box is full of old friends. I haven't looked in that box for years and years," said Grandpa.

"Old friends?" questioned Jack. "Are you talking about the pictures of the army men?"

"Yep, they were my buddies. We fought together in the war," answered Grandpa. "Will you tell me about 'em?" Jack asked. Grandpa shook his head from side to side without saying a word.

"Will you pleeeease tell me about 'em, Grandpa?" begged Jack. "Grandpa, is that you standing next to the jeep?"

"That's me, Jack," answered Grandpa. While Grandpa was answering his questions, Jack kept digging in the box. He found an envelope with a rubber band around it keeping something hard inside. As he took the rubber band off, he said, "You've never told me about the war, Grandpa."

"I don't talk about it much because some of my buddies didn't make it home," said Grandpa. "What do you mean they didn't make it home?" asked Jack. "They died in battle and were buried over there. They gave up their lives fighting for our freedom," answered Grandpa. "They must have been mighty brave men," Jack replied. "Yes, they were," answered Grandpa.

Jack opened the envelope to find a silver star attached to a ribbon. "This looks important, Grandpa." Tears filled Grandpa's eyes when he saw the medal in Jack's hand. "Is it yours? Are you a hero?" asked Jack in rapid-fire succession. The single tear in grandpa's eye became a flood of tears that rolled down his face.

"I got that for pulling some guys out of danger, but that didn't make me a hero," said Grandpa. "My buddies were real heroes, patriots."

"What's a patriot, Grandpa?" asked Jack. "A patriot is someone who loves his country. He does his part to keep America a great nation by being a good citizen," answered Grandpa. "How can I be a patriot, Grandpa?" Grandpa's tears slowed as he answered his little grandson's big question. "You can start by showing respect for the *Stars and Stripes*." He reached out and touched the flag hanging from his porch.

Jack ran over and touched the flag, too. "I've learned a lot about how to take care of the flag at school, Grandpa." "I'm glad to hear that, Jack," said Grandpa. "I fold this flag every night and hang it out every morning. I never let it touch the ground."

"We learned that rule at school, but I've never met anyone who did it, till you, Grandpa," said Jack with a grin on his face. "I want to learn more about how to be a patriot. Will you teach me?"

"It would be my honor, Jack," said Grandpa, taking great pride in his grandson. For the next few months Grandpa made sure Jack learned all the words to "The Star Spangled Banner." Together they practiced standing at attention with hands over their hearts at baseball games. Grandpa smiled every time he saw someone in the stands look at his little patriot with his hand over his heart trying to sing the words to our national anthem. Jack smiled every time he saw others put their hands over their hearts too.

Jack couldn't wait till the 4th of July parade because of all that Grandpa had taught him about loving his country. Jack spent the night with Grandpa the night before the big parade.

The next morning, Jack and Grandpa waited for the parade to come by. When Grandpa saw the flag, he thought about all the stories he had shared with Jack about his war days. When Jack saw the flag, he jumped to his feet, and said, "Grandpa, stand up!"

22 Respecting Our Country

Grandpa raised his tired old bones out of his chair and stood next to Jack who was standing proudly with his hand over his heart. As Jack looked down the sidewalk, he saw others begin to stand at attention. All but Sergeant Joe, one of Grandpa's friends, who was sitting in a wheelchair in his army uniform. He was trying to stand up, but couldn't quite do it.

Jack knew he needed help, so he ran over to the old gentleman and said, "Lean on me, Sergeant Joe. I'll help you stand." With Jack's help, the Sergeant stood tall and saluted the flag. Jack's grandpa made his way over to stand with them. He put his arm around Jack and dropped his champion marble in Jack's blue jean pocket as he patted him on the head.

Grandpa smiled with pride as he stood next to his little patriot with a big heart.

Just the beginning...

Day 2   MUSIC OF THE HEART®

1. Play the video for your class.
2. Discussion questions:
   - *In which war did Francis Scott Key write the National Anthem?*
     The War of 1812 between the United States and Britain
   - *What is the name of the fort on the Baltimore Harbor?*
     Fort McHenry
   - *Where was Francis Scott Key during the battle? Why?*
     He was on a British ship because he was helping to free one of his friends.
   - *Can you describe the flag?*
     It was huge! It was 30ft by 42ft! Handmade by Mary Pickersgill and her daughter. It could be seen in the early morning and signaled that the U.S. had won the Battle of Fort McHenry.
3. Practice singing the *National Anthem* until you know all the words!

You'll Need:
- Video: *The History of the American National Anthem* (https://youtu.be/IVaIjnS-Br10)

Day 3   WRITING FROM THE HEART

Ask your students to consider the following journal prompt and answer it according to your classroom writing requirements:

What do you think it would be like to live in a country where there is very little freedom?

You'll Need:
- **Respecting Our Country** activity sheet (1/student)

Days 2-5

Day 4 — CREATIVE CONNECTION

1. Play a recording of the *National Anthem* as students follow and sing along with the lyric sheet.

2. Discussion:
   - *Where do we hear our National Anthem?*
     Sporting events, patriotic events, parades
   - *What is the name of our National Anthem?*
     "The Star-Spangled Banner"
   - *Can you remember who wrote the "Star-Spangled Banner"?*
     Francis Scott Key
   - *When you hear the words, how do you think he felt when he wrote them?*
     He wasn't certain who had won the battle, but when the smoke cleared and the flag was still there, he was proud that America had won.
   - *How do you feel when you hear it?* (Answers will vary)
   - *Why is America known as the "land of the free"?*
     Americans have many freedoms that people in other countries do not have. We have the freedom to worship as we like, the freedom to have privacy in our homes, the freedom to receive an education, etc.
   - *Why is America the "home of the brave"?*
     Brave people came to this country to start a new life and many have fought for us to continue to have freedom.
   - *Do you know someone who has fought in a war for our country? How might you show your patriotism to someone who is a veteran?*
     By saluting or clapping for someone in uniform. By saying "thank you" to someone in uniform.

You'll Need:
- Recording of the *National Anthem* on YouTube or other digital source
- **Star-Spangled Banner Lyrics** activity sheet

Day 5 — TECH TIME

Interactive Whiteboard Activity on MyManners Portal

Use your keyboard to show a soldier just how much you respect them!

MANNERS IN ACTION

Whooooo will hang the **Happle** this week?

PATRIOTISM—Loving our country enough to protect it and the principles upon which it was founded

CITIZENSHIP—An attitude of cooperation and social responsibility

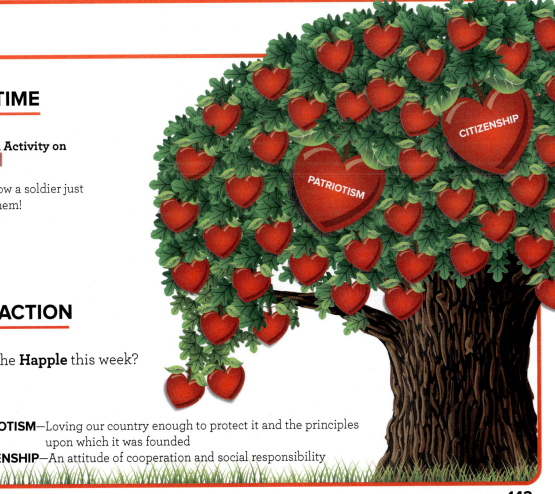

WEEK 23
RESPECTING OUR ENVIRONMENT

Big Ideas

- Teaching children to respect their environment helps to instill an appreciation for what they have.

- Learning to conserve our resources encourages children to be creative and inventive, which develops their imagination.

- Children learn they have a part to play in keeping our environment clean so everyone can enjoy the beauty of our world.

For Your Heart

Respecting our environment is something we do not only for ourselves, but also for those who come after us. Learning what we can do on a personal level to protect our land, water and air helps improve our quality of life and demonstrates to others that we care how our actions impact *their* quality of life.

The EPA recommends "3R's" of waste reduction: Reduce the amount of products we use, Reuse the products we have and Recycle the products we do use. You can help the next generation take a different view of our natural resources and the way we use them. Teach them that living with less is really living with more.

Dr. Seuss had a simple solution in *The Lorax*...reach the next generation with a message that would open their eyes to see they could help the environment. In his personal favorite book, he told children, "Unless someone like you cares a whole awful lot, nothing is going to get better. It's not."

For the Hearts of Your Students

When children learn to respect the environment, they build knowledge and develop skills necessary to address complex environmental issues. By helping your students develop a different way of looking at our environment in their younger years, you will help them form responsible consumption habits as they grow.

In this week's lesson, you will encourage your students to be *conscientious* as they recognize the importance of being careful with their possessions and not wasteful with our natural resources. Learning how to reduce and reuse products, your students discover they can make up their own fun by being *resourceful*. They'll thank you for helping them develop ingenuity!

You have an opportunity to educate a generation of new "MacGyvers" who will be equipped to creatively solve our society's environmental problems one day when it's their turn to take over.

23 Respecting Our Environment

CONSCIENTIOUS—Diligently careful

RESOURCEFUL—Finding creative solutions to everyday problems; using your imagination and mind to repurpose materials

REMEMBER

SKILLS AND OBJECTIVES

- Children will consider what it means to show respect for our environment and protect its beauty.
- Children will learn the symbols and meaning of "Reduce, Reuse and Recycle."
- Children will learn the practical application of "Reduce, Reuse and Recycle."

Here Comes the Garbage Barge!
by Jonah Winter

How far would you be willing to go to dump your trash?

GUIDING CHILDREN'S LEARNING

1. Begin the lesson by introducing the *Heart Attributes* for the week, CONSCIENTIOUS and RESOURCEFUL.

2. It's Story Time! Read aloud or listen to the recording of *For the Love of the Sea*

3. After the story, lead your students in the following discussion:
    - *Who rescued Tommy after his raft capsized?*
      Cap'n Nick
    - *What was Tommy trying to see when he went out on his raft?*
      The coral reef
    - *How did Tommy discover the trash on the bottom of the sea?*
      Cap'n Nick let him use his snorkeling goggles and held him over the side of his boat so he could view the reef. The trash was stuck in the reef.
    - *Where did all the garbage come from?*
      From all of us! From people like you and me.
    - *What community project did Tommy start in Merryville?*
      Fishing for trash from the sea and clearing the trash from the beaches.
    - *How did the trash become treasure?*
      In addition to the jewelry and vases, money was made from recycling some of the trash to help others in Merryville.

MANNERS IN ACTION

1. Review the definitions of the *Heart Attributes*, CONSCIENTIOUS and RESOURCEFUL. Remind students that these are the last two *Heart Attributes* of the school year. Ask them to consider which *Heart Attributes* they have grown the most in this year!

2. Discuss these *Big Ideas* with your students:
    - *The environment around us is naturally beautiful.*
    - *We can be RESOURCEFUL and turn trash into treasure.*
    - *We must be CONSCIENTIOUS to restore the beauty of the environment and to keep it that way.*

3. This is the last *Manners in Action* of the school year! As your students put their manners into action, ask them how they will make an effort this week to show respect for the environment. Have them share their experiences on Day 5 as they hang the last **Happles** on the **Happle Tree**.

Day 1

FOR THE LOVE OF THE SEA

Once upon a heart in Merryville, all Tommy could hear was his own panting and the crashing of the waves growing more intense. He struggled under the weight of his precious cargo. He wiped the sweat from his forehead. At last, he felt the sea foam lick his bare feet as he drew in a big gulp the cool, salty air.

Finally, he thought. Tommy put the nose of his homemade raft into the first wave and climbed in. He was proud of the little boat he had built on his own. Carefully, nervously, he paddled farther and farther out. *You're fine, you can swim*, he told himself. His little craft climbed over the first wave, the second, the third—*Nooooooooo! Nooooooooooo!*

All at once, his little boat tilted sideways and capsized. He closed his eyes and felt the cold water rush all around him. Panicked, he kicked to the surface and gasped. He turned in circles frantically for a moment. *Where's the shore? Where IS it?* He couldn't see the beach over the crest of the waves.

Suddenly, a big, strong hand grabbed the back of his shirt. Up out of the water he was lifted and plopped into a bobbing, wooden boat. There was stinging salt water in his eyes. Someone gave him a towel and wrapped him in a dense, warm blanket.

"There, there," he heard a gravelly voice saying, "many a young man's taken that tumble and been braver for it. You'll be righter than a main mast just as soon as you catch your breath."

Tommy rubbed his eyes clear. He blinked a couple times in the bright sunlight and there, with two long oars in his mighty hands, was Cap'n Nick, the suntanned, weather-beaten pirate.

"Cap'n Nick! You saved me!" Tommy jumped toward the captain and wrapped his arms around the crusty sailor's neck. The hardy man shook with a deep, warm laugh like only seafarers can.

Tommy was just glad to be safe again. He looked around for his raft. Cap'n Nick had strung it up to his own, stronger vessel, beaten up as it was.

"Where were you headed without a first mate, little captain?" Cap'n Nick asked, rowing the boat along with the gray-green waves.

"I wanted to see the reef! They say that people from far away travel all the way to Merryville just to see it!"

"Well now, you only had to say so!" Cap'n Nick smiled with a twinkle in his eye. With just a couple of oar strokes, Cap'n Nick rowed them out farther. Tommy clinched the side until his knuckles glowed white. He didn't want to slip in again.

Cap'n Nick rummaged through a worn-out chest and drew out a pair of snorkeling goggles.

"See for yourself!" Cap'n Nick held onto the back of Tommy's shirt, which instantly made him feel safe. With a big breath, Tommy decided to take the plunge. He dunked his head under the surface and opened his eyes. Right before him exploded an underwater, rainbow paradise.

The coral reef was enormous—like a giant, multicolored mountain sunken beneath the ocean's surface. *Am I on a different planet?* Tommy thought.

Schools of glimmering fish swam right by his outstretched hands. They looked like someone had spilled whole treasure chests of jewels—sky blue, sunflower yellow, neon orange. Eels that seemed to go on forever slithered in and out of little pockets in the white stone. In the distance, he caught sight of what seemed like an enormous dark square. It bent backward and forward and drew closer. Almost at his fingertips, glided a gigantic manta ray, the size of at least two of his dad's trucks put together!

But upon closer examination, Tommy saw shimmering metal that was not so beautiful. There, in the midst of the rainforest of the sea, were piles of bottles and cans lodged in the base of the coral garden. Not unlike litter that was sometimes scattered on the streets of Merryville, debris had drifted through the waters to find an unwelcome home in the reef.

"Cap'n Nick, Cap'n Nick," Tommy gasped as he came up for air. "What happened down there? Where did all the garbage come from?"

"From folks just like you and me, Tommy."

"We have to do something!" shouted Tommy.

"Tommy, my nets fill up every day with a few fish and a lot of everything else," answered the troubled Cap'n. "I do all I can to help the sea I love so much, but I'm losing the battle. I need help."

"Count me in, Cap'n. I'll recruit my friends, too."

The next day looked like roll call at the beach. Miguel, Wesley, Sarah, Terrell, Emma, Jerome, Jasmine, Guiming, Tyranne and many town folk gathered to come up with creative ideas for cleaning up the sea.

"Rather than fish for food, let's set aside a day every week to fish for trash! We can drag nets along the surface of

23 Respecting Our Environment

the water to capture bottles and cans," Jerome shared with great excitement.

"Yeah, and when the tide tolls in, we can take turns patrolling the beach to collect the stuff that washes up on shore," added Sarah.

"But what will we do with it all?" asked Caroline.

"We could make jewelry from pieces of glass and flower vases from old bottles," Sarah said.

"Hey," shouted Tommy, "we could turn in the aluminum cans for cash and make the money count for something."

In the weeks ahead, folks, filled the back of Ol' McDonald's pickup truck with debris from the sea, and even traded some of it for cash...lots of cash!

The gathering of rubbish from the sea—lost, tossed and forgotten—captured the hearts and turned the minds of Merryville's volunteers to citizens who had likewise been forgotten in the community.

It didn't take long before the Veterans' Home got a fresh coat of paint. One of Merryville's oldest citizens got a new roof. Sergeant Joe was given a new wheelchair. And Tommy and his friends hand-delivered old bottles filled with flowers for the residents of the Sunrise Retirement Home.

Aye! The trash now be treasure in Merryville! mused Cap'n Nick.

Just the beginning...

Day 2   ART OF THE HEART®

1. Distribute activity sheets and explain that this is the symbol for **Reduce, Reuse, Recycle**.
2. Write the three words on the blanks.
3. *What does REDUCE mean? What can we REDUCE?*
   - Reduce means to limit the use of.
   - Reduce the use of disposable water bottles.
   - Turn off lights when you leave a room.
   - Walk or bicycle to places if you can, to save gas.
   - Use both sides of a sheet of paper.

   What does REUSE mean? What can we REUSE?
   - Reuse means to use something again.
   - Give clothes and furniture to a thrift store.
   - Use glass jars as vases or for storing items.
   - Reuse plastic bags around your home or bring them to the grocery store.

   What does RECYCLE mean? What can we RECYCLE?
   - Recycle means to allow an item to be turned into a new item.
   - Never throw paper, glass, aluminum or plastic into the trash or on the ground.
   - Recycle any item that has a symbol on it.
   - Always recycle batteries and electronics. Bring them to a local electronics store.

   Does your family Reduce, Reuse and Recycle?
   - Some of the resources we use are limited— trees, fresh water, oil and gas. We need to protect our environment and do our part!
4. Ask students to bring an item from home with the symbol on it for Day 4!

> **You'll Need:**
> - **Reduce, Reuse, Recycle** activity sheet (1/student)

Days 2-5

Day 3 WRITING FROM THE HEART

Ask your students to consider the following journal prompt and answer it according to your classroom writing requirements:

Have you thought about where the trash goes? Describe what happens to everything you throw away!

You'll Need:
- Respecting Our Environment activity sheet (1/student)

Day 4 CREATIVE CONNECTION

1. Gather the items with the **Reduce, Reuse, Recycle** symbol on them.
2. Students may research individually or as a group to discover what the symbol means.
3. Have students write down their findings and report to the class.

You'll Need:
- What Does It Mean activity sheet
- Recyclable items from home

Day 5 TECH TIME

Interactive Whiteboard Activity on MyManners Portal

Only you can save Recycle City with your knowledge!

MANNERS IN ACTION

Whooooo will hang the **Happle** this week?

CONSCIENTIOUS—Diligently careful
RESOURCEFUL—Finding creative solutions to everyday problems; using your imagination and mind to repurpose materials

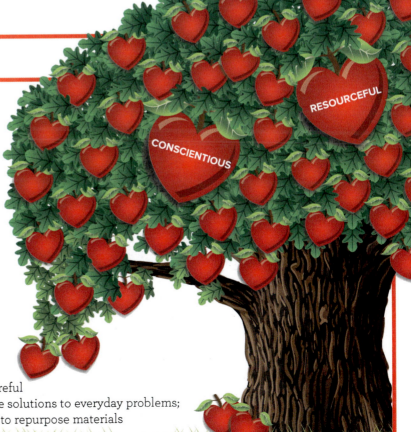

The Education *of* the HEART must be *the* HEART *of* Education

WILBUR'S GLOSSARY

A

ACCEPTANCE
Treating everyone you meet with the same respect, regardless of differences

APPRECIATION
Recognizing and acknowledging value in people, places and things

APPROPRIATE
Knowing the right thing to say or do in any given situation

C

CITIZENSHIP
An attitude of cooperation and social responsibility

CIVIL
To respect others and self for the betterment of community

CONSCIENTIOUS
Diligently careful

CONSIDERATE
Taking into account the feelings of others before you speak or act

COOPERATION
Working with others for everyone's best; choosing to be helpful, not hurtful

COURTESY
Respectful and well-mannered words and actions toward others

E

EMPATHY
Walking in another person's shoes

ENCOURAGEMENT
Offering words to others to build their confidence

WILBUR'S GLOSSARY

EXPRESSIVE
Revealing the content of your heart

F

FORGIVENESS
Choosing to let go of bad feelings toward another person

FRIENDLINESS
Welcoming others by offering a quick smile and a kind word

G

GENEROSITY
Gladly giving my time, talent and treasure

GENTLE
Speaking and acting with tenderness

GOODNESS
Being kind, compassionate, and forgiving

GRACIOUS
Being polite, understanding and generous in all situations

GRATEFUL
Giving thanks from the heart

H

HONOR
Valuing the worth of another by showing respect

HOSPITALITY
Serving others so they feel cared for and comfortable

HUMBLE CONFIDENCE
The courage to be my best so that I can help others become their best

HUMILITY
Not caring who gets credit

WILBUR'S GLOSSARY

K

KINDNESS
Showing care for others in an unexpected and exceptional way

L

LOVE
Genuinely caring for others

LOYALTY
Faithful devotion

M

MANNERS
An attitude of the heart that puts the needs of others ahead of my own

MATURITY
The ability to make the right choice in spite of negative influences

O

OBEDIENCE
Choosing to submit to authority

P

PARTICIPATION
Choosing to be fully involved in the task or project at hand

PATIENCE
Even-tempered endurance

PATRIOTISM
Loving our country enough to protect it and the principles upon which it was founded

POLITE
Using kind words and actions in all situations

WILBUR'S GLOSSARY

R

RESOURCEFUL
Finding creative solutions to everyday problems; using your imagination and mind to repurpose materials

RESPECT
Treating others with dignity

RESPONSIBILITY
Following through on your duties without supervision

S

SELF-CONTROL
The ability to manage yourself when no one is looking

SELF-ESTEEM
Self-absorption, presenting itself as self-conceit on one extreme and self-consciousness on the other

SELF-RESPECT
A character trait that results from treating others with dignity

SELFLESS
Choosing to give without thinking of what someone will give back to you

SPORTSMANSHIP
Being more concerned with supporting your team than helping yourself

T

THOUGHTFUL
Looking for ways to make others feel loved

TRUSTWORTHY
Doing what you said you would do when you said you would do it

U

UNDERSTANDING
Looking at others and listening to others without judgment

REPRODUCIBLES

STUDENT ACTIVITY SHEETS

Week 1	156, 157, 158, 159
Week 2	160, 161, 162
Week 3	163, 164
Week 4	165, 166
Week 5	167
Week 6	168, 169, 170
Week 7	171, 172, 173
Week 8	174, 175, 176
Week 9	177, 178, 179
Week 10	180, 181, 182
Week 11	183, 184, 185
Week 12	186, 187, 188
Week 13	189, 190
Week 14	191, 192, 193
Week 15	194
Week 16	195, 196, 197
Week 17	198, 199
Week 18	200, 201
Week 19	202, 203
Week 20	204
Week 21	205, 206, 207
Week 22	208, 209
Week 23	210, 211, 212

HOME CONNECTION LETTERS

Week 1	213
Week 2	214
Week 3	215
Week 4	216
Week 5	217
Week 6	218
Week 7	219
Week 8	220
Week 9	221
Week 10	222
Week 11	223
Week 12	224
Week 13	225
Week 14	226
Week 15	227
Week 16	228
Week 17	229
Week 18	230
Week 19	231
Week 20	232
Week 21	233
Week 22	234
Week 23	235

Student Activity Sheet - Week 1

Map of Merryville

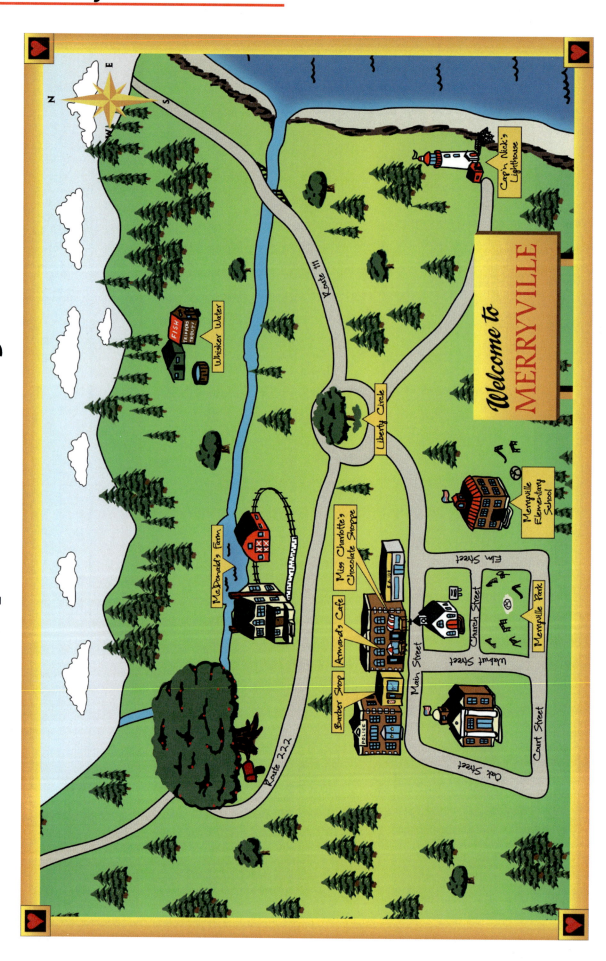

Student Activity Sheet - Week 1

My Merryville

Name

157

Student Activity Sheet - Week 1

Welcome to Merryville

When you are looking for a friend, what Heart Attribute do you think is most important? Why?

Name

Student Activity Sheet - Week 1

Manners in the Heart

Name

Student Activity Sheet - Week 2

Good Deeds

> You will be creating a Class Constitution with your classmates. To begin this process, write down your own ideas as to which rules and attitudes are the most important.

WORDS
How should we speak to one another?

_____

_____

_____

ACTIONS
How should we behave ourselves at school?

_____

_____

_____

ATTITUDES
What attitudes in our hearts should govern our words and actions?

_____

_____

_____

Name

Student Activity Sheet - Week 2

Introducing Good Deeds

Rules and laws are written for everyone's good. If you could write only one rule for the good of everyone in your classroom, what would it be? Tell why.

_____

_____

_____

_____

_____

_____

_____

_____

_____

_____

_____

_____

_____

_____

_____

_____

Name

Student Activity Sheet - Week 2

Class Constitution

We the Students...

Student Activity Sheet - Week 3

Seeds of Respect

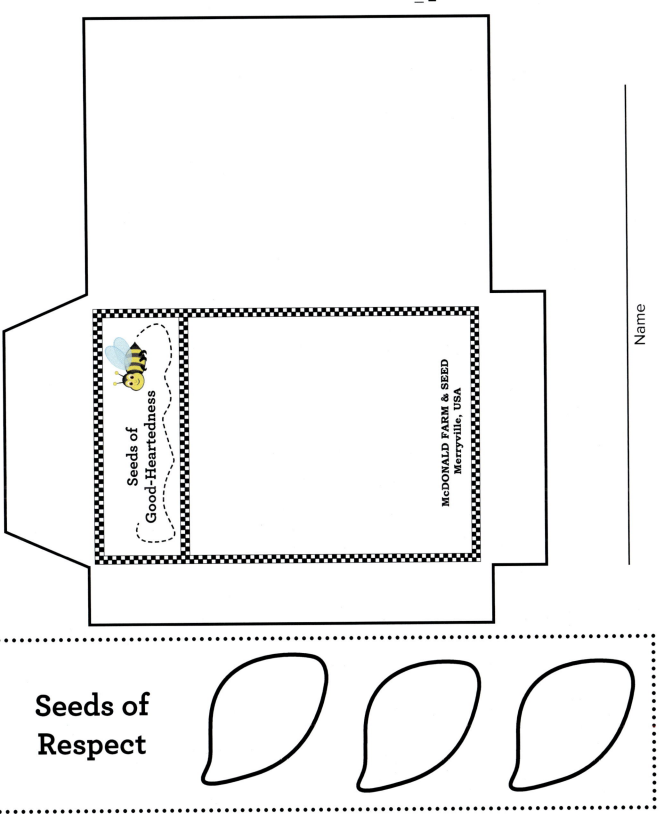

Student Activity Sheet - Week 3

Choosing Respect

Describe a time that you saw someone being bullied or treated with disrespect. How did it make you feel?

Name

Student Activity Sheet - Week 4

Helping Others

Think about someone outside your family who helps you. Describe who they are and what they do to help you. Why do you think they choose to help you?

Name

Student Activity Sheet - Week 4

Helping You and Me

Think of those who help you! Describe *how* they help you and what you can begin to do for them!

People who help me	How they help me	How can I help them?

_____

Name

Student Activity Sheet - Week 5

My Forgiveness Pledge

I, _____, will forgive the person who hurt me.
      (NAME)

I understand that forgiveness...

- Means I let go of the angry feelings
  I have toward the person who has hurt me.

- Is good for my heart,
  not just good for the person who needs forgiving.

- Is good for my heart,
  so it is also good for me and the other people in my life.

- Does not always mean...
  I have to trust that same person in the same way in the future.

_____   _____
(DATE)   (NAME)

Student Activity Sheet - Week 6

My Treasure Chest

Color and cut out the treasure chest. Fold on the dotted lines to make a pocket that will hold the hearts of gold. Staple the edges of the chest closed.

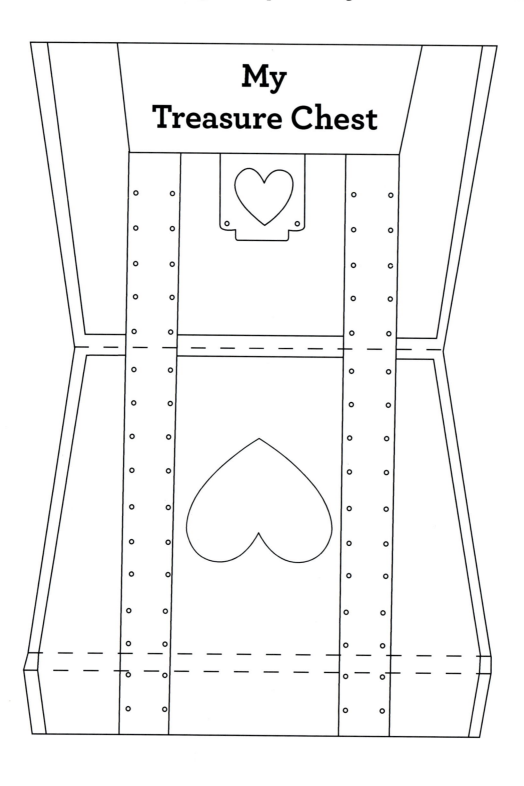

Hearts of Gold

Color the hearts on one side and cut them out.
Then write words of encouragement on the opposite side.

Student Activity Sheet - Week 6

Appreciating Others

Think about someone in your family and describe three things you appreciate about them.

Name

Student Activity Sheet - Week 7

Don't Stand Back

Don't Stand Back

Don't stand back, — Take one step back.
Step in. — Step forward as you lean over.
Stand up! — Stand tall with hands raised over your head.

Don't let that bully beat him up! — Wave your hands in a "no" motion. Hands on hip (with a bad 'attitude') at the word bully. End by punching your fists in front of you.

Fill his heart with all the good stuff — Make a pouring motion into the heart with both hands.

Then that bully won't be so tough! — Turn in one full circle, back to center. End with hands folded in front across the chest (with a good 'attitude') and SMILE!

_____
Name

Student Activity Sheet - Week 7

Being a Buddy, Not a Bully

Can you think of a time you could have stood up for someone who was being bullied, but did not? Is it easy to stand up and step in when someone is being bullied? Why or why not?

Name

Student Activity Sheet - Week 7

Bully & Buddy

Fill each heart with words describing what is in the heart of a BUDDY and a BULLY.

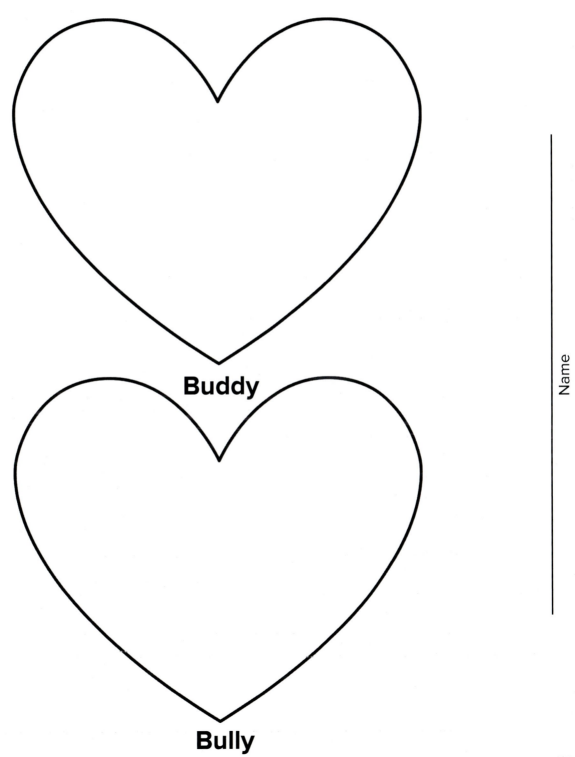

Buddy

Bully

Name

Student Activity Sheet - Week 8

Wilbur's Glasses

Color and cut out the glasses, then glue an arm to each side of the glasses.

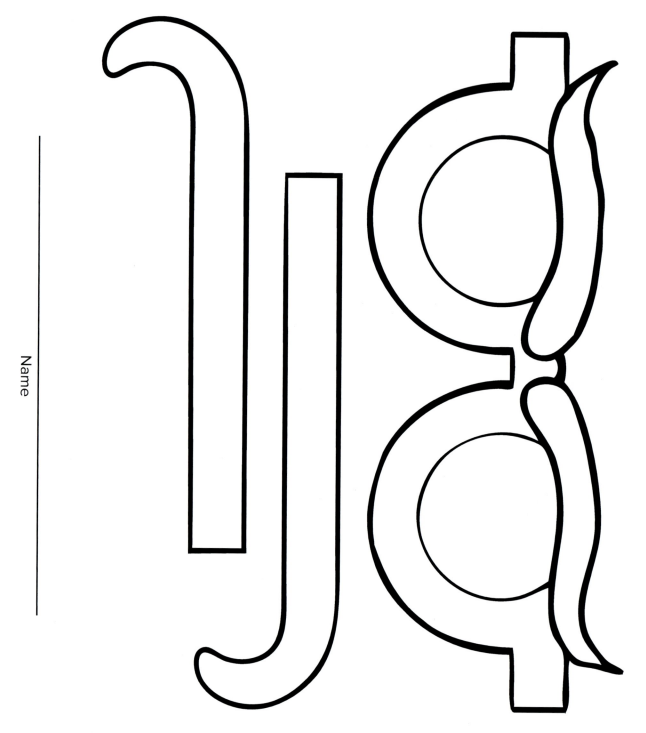

Name

Student Activity Sheet - Week 8

Following the Golden Rule

Treating others the way I want to be treated means...

Name

Student Activity Sheet - Week 8

What's on the Inside Shows on the Outside

Put your glasses on to look into the heart and circle the correct answers.

LOVE	HUG or HIT
PATIENCE	WHINE or WAIT
KINDNESS	HELP or HURT
SADNESS	CRY or LAUGH
ANGER	HUG or HIT
SELF-CONTROL	TALK or LISTEN
JOY	SMILE or FROWN
SELFISHNESS	TAKE or GIVE

Name

Student Activity Sheet - Week 9

GENTLEMAN

MY CODE OF HONOR

As a gentleman,
I promise from this day forward to...

Open the door for ladies and adults.

Stop in a doorway to allow a girl to enter first.

Stand when a girl comes to the table.

Stand when a girl leaves the table.

Offer to help a girl carry heavy things.

Give up my seat to a girl or an adult.

Remove my hat indoors, especially in the presence of ladies.

Open the car door for girls and ladies.

Pull out a girl's or lady's chair for dinner.

Never, never use curse words.

_____   _____
NAME   DATE

Student Activity Sheet - Week 9

LADY

MY CODE OF HONOR

As a lady,
I promise from this day forward to...

Open the door for adults.

Never say mean things about someone else.

Offer to help an elderly person carry heavy things.

Offer to help an older person in any way he or she needs help.

Give up my seat to an elderly person.

Open the car door for an elderly person.

Never, never use curse words.

Say "thank you" to a boy when he treats me like a lady.

Be kind to others at all times.

NAME   DATE

Student Activity Sheet - Week 9

Becoming Ladies and Gentlemen

Do you think acting like ladies and gentlemen is just for adults? Why would it be good to learn these manners as a third grader?

Name

Student Activity Sheet - Week 10

Being a Host

Unscramble these words to help remember how to be a good host!

1. Always _____ permission before inviting someone over.
   k s a

2. Find out what _____ your guest likes before they come over.
   o d o f

3. Don't change your _____ after inviting your guest!
   n d i m

4. _____ your guest at the door.
   r t e g e

5. Always _____ up after you make a mess!
   c i p k

6. Give your _____ first choice when deciding what to do.
   t g e s u

7. Offer them something to _____ and _____.
   t e a   n i r k d

8. Walk your guest to the _____ when they are ready to _____.
   r o d o   e e l v a

9. _____ your guest for coming over!
   t n a k h

10. Thank your family for letting you get together with a _____.
    n f i r d e

_____
Name

Student Activity Sheet - Week 10

Party Planning

You are hosting a party for someone special and this is your chance to IMAGINE the greatest party ever for them. Brainstorm your ideas below:

Who is the guest of honor at your party?

What are you celebrating?

Where will the party be?

Name a date and time for your party.

Will you have a theme?

How do you want your guests to dress?

What will you eat and drink?

What will you and your guests do?

_____
Name

Student Activity Sheet - Week 10

You're Invited...

Cut out and create an invitation for the greatest party you can imagine! Use the Party Planning activity sheet from Day 3 and fill in the blanks. Fold it over and decorate the front of the invitation with a drawing and the words, "You're Invited!"

Guest of Honor _____

When and Where _____

Food and Drink _____

Fun stuff we're going to do!!! _____

_____

Student Activity Sheet - Week 11

A GOOD GUEST SAYS

A good guest always says…

_____
Name

183

Student Activity Sheet - Week 11

Being a Guest

Think about these words: Hello, Please, Thank you, and Goodbye. Which do you think is the most important? Why? (Hint: there is not a right or wrong answer!)

Name

Student Activity Sheet - Week 11

Thank You Card

Cut out the card and fold it in half. Draw a picture on the front.
On the inside, write: Thank You! Love, (your name).

Student Activity Sheet - Week 12

See, Smile, Step, Shake, Speak!

Cut out the squares below. Mix them up. Put them in the correct order on your desk.

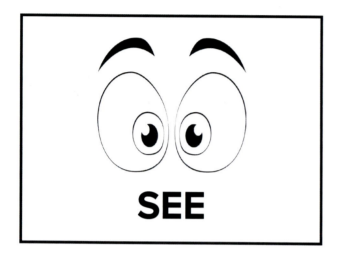
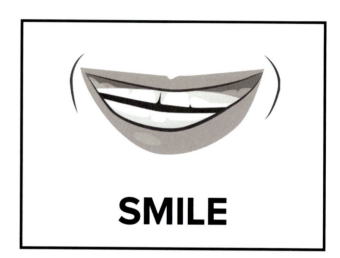
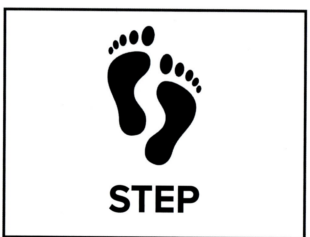

Student Activity Sheet - Week 12

Greetings and Introductions

Is it easy or hard for you to meet new people? Give an example.

Name

Student Activity Sheet - Week 12

Five Steps to Making a GOOD First Impression!

Fill in the blanks to learn how to show respect to adults!

SEE—make eye contact

SMILE—as you look the person in the eyes

STEP—toward the person, or lean in a little if you are already close

SHAKE—palm to palm and firm (but not so firm that you hurt the other person!)

SPEAK—"It's nice to meet you!" and then ask a question

☑ **GOOD First Impression?** ☒ **BAD First Impression?**

- ☐ Looking someone in the eye.
- ☐ Smiling.
- ☐ Fidgeting and not wanting to answer questions.
- ☐ Asking the other person questions.
- ☐ Thinking about something else when you're with someone.
- ☐ Saying something rude.
- ☐ Listening to the other person.
- ☐ Sighing and rolling your eyes if the other person says something incorrect.
- ☐ Not shaking hands with someone.
- ☐ Seeing someone and stepping toward them with a smile.
- ☐ Hiding behind someone else so you don't have to talk.
- ☐ Shaking hands with someone you are meeting for the first time.

_____
Name

Student Activity Sheet - Week 13

Let's Get Started!

Read these following conversation starters. Come up with two questions of your own!

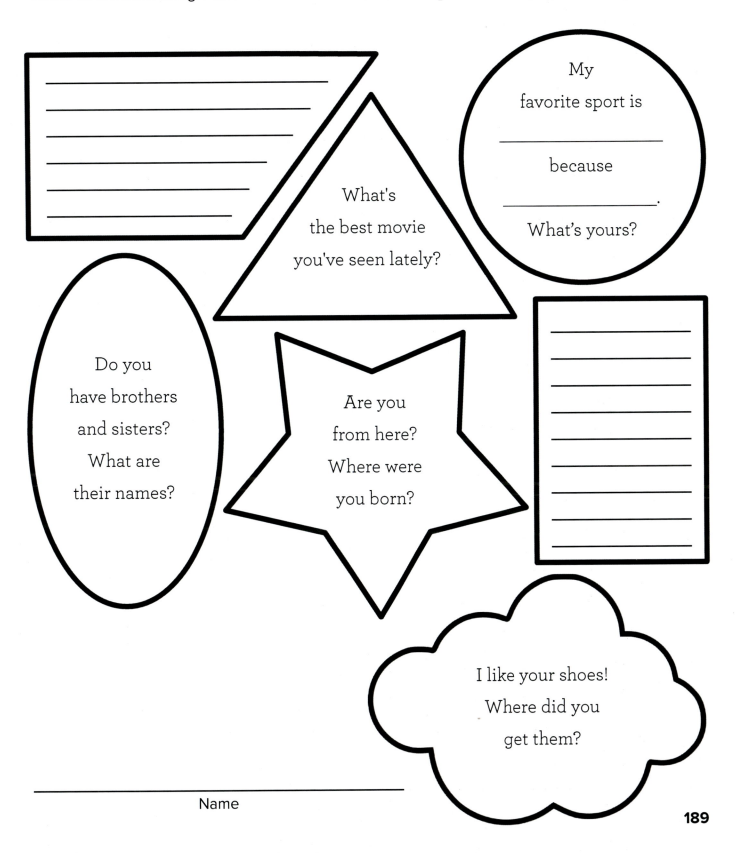

My favorite sport is _____ because _____. What's yours?

What's the best movie you've seen lately?

Do you have brothers and sisters? What are their names?

Are you from here? Where were you born?

I like your shoes! Where did you get them?

Name _____

189

Student Activity Sheet - Week 13

Encouraging Conversation

What do you most LOVE talking about? Tell us more!

Name

Student Activity Sheet - Week 14

NO PHONE ZONE! #1

Describe the no phone zones!

Name

Student Activity Sheet - Week 14

Using the Phone

Describe a time you wished someone was paying attention to you rather than to their phone.

Name

Student Activity Sheet - Week 14

NO PHONE ZONE! #2

Draw a NO PHONE ZONE! Sign and start your own campaign for wise cell phone use.

Name

Student Activity Sheet - Week 15

Model Letter and Envelope

Use this model letter and envelope to create a personal letter for someone special!

_____ (Date)

Dear _____,

_____

_____

_____

_____

_____

Sincerely,

_____ (Name)

Your Name
Your Street Address
City, State Zip Code

Place Stamp Here

Recipient's Name
Recipient's Street Address
City, State Zip Code

Student Activity Sheet - Week 16

ADULTS

Fill in the blanks to show how ADULTS should be treated.

A __ __ __ __ __ questions.

D __ __ what they say.

U __ __ their correct title.

L __ __ __ __ __ and look them in the eye.

T __ __ __ your frown upside down.

S __ __ "Sir" and "Ma'am."

Leaders in Government

Name those serving in elected offices of leadership for your city, state and country.

The mayor of my city is Mayor _____.

The governor of my state is Governor _____.

The president of my country is President _____.

_____
Name

195

Student Activity Sheet - Week 16

Respecting Adults

If you could meet any president from any time in history, who would you like to meet? What would you want to ask him?

_____
Name

Student Activity Sheet - Week 16

Thank You Note

Write a note to an elected official. Don't forget to sign your name!

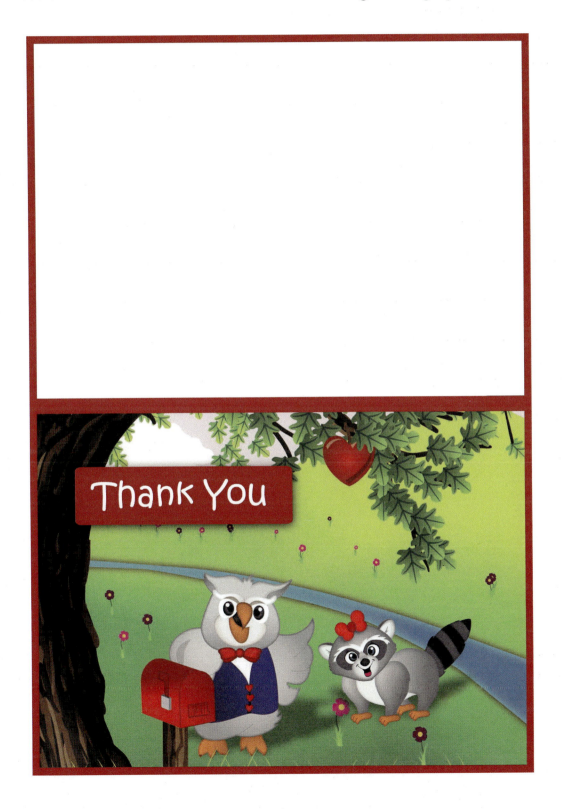

Student Activity Sheet - Week 17

Badge of Honor

Color the star blue, the circle yellow, and the strips blue. Cut out the shapes.
Glue the yellow circle to the center of the blue star.
Glue the two "ribbons" in place on the back of the badge.

Student Activity Sheet - Week 17

Respecting the Team

Are you usually a good sport or a bad sport? Explain.

Name

Student Activity Sheet - Week 18

Countries of the World

Find the country names in the word search!

ARGENTINA
BRAZIL
DENMARK
FIJI
INDIA
NORWAY
SPAIN

AUSTRALIA
CANADA
EGYPT
FRANCE
IRELAND
PORTUGAL
TURKEY

BELGIUM
CHILE
ENGLAND
GERMANY
JAPAN
SINGAPORE

Name

Student Activity Sheet - Week 18

Respecting Differences

If you could visit any country in the world, which one would you choose to visit? Why?

_____

Name

Student Activity Sheet - Week 19

No Gossip Allowed!

Fill in the blanks on your own and then discuss with your class.

Gossip is _____ about someone else.

Gossip is saying things about _____ else that aren't nice.

Gossip may or may not be _____.

Gossip can ruin _____.

If someone gossips, ask them how they would _____ if someone said something unkind about them.

_____ away if they do not stop spreading gossip.

Never repeat gossip that you _____.

---

	feel	walk	true	wrong
hear	talking		friendships	someone

Student Activity Sheet - Week 19

Respecting Privacy

Why do you think gossip hurts friendships?

Name

Student Activity Sheet - Week 20

Respecting Property

How do you feel when you get a really good grade on a test? Would you feel differently if you had cheated to get that grade?

Name

Student Activity Sheet - Week 21

Just Act Respectfully

If there is a long line in a store, how should you wait in the line? Show me!	Show me the kind of voice you should use when at the mall...	What should you say if a store clerk asks if she can help you?	How should you behave in the dressing room? Show me!
What should you do with clothing after you have looked at it or tried it on?	If someone in the mall asks you a question, how should you answer?	I want two people to act out respectfully buying something in the store. One of you will be the sales clerk and the other will be the shopper. The rest of us will tell you what you did well and what you can work on.	Should you walk or run in the mall?
When there is a crowd of people in the mall that you need to get through, you do not shove, but say...	What should you do if you lose the adult you are with when at the mall?	When getting on the elevator, do you first wait for people to get off? Act this out for me.	Show me how you should ride on the elevator or escalator...
If you accidentally spill your drink or food in the food court, you should...	What should you do after finishing your food in the food court?	Is it okay to bring food or drink into a store?	When walking through the mall, it is very important to _____ where you are going! Why?

Student Activity Sheet - Week 21

Just Act Respectfully

Teacher's Key

If there is a long line in a store, how should you wait in the line? Show me! **Quietly, without moving around and with a smile.**	Show me the kind of voice you should use when at the mall... **Your inside voice! (No yelling!)**	What should you say if a store clerk asks if she can help you? **Smile and say "Yes, please!" or "No, thank you, ma'am!"**	How should you behave in the dressing room? Show me! **No goofing around, talk quietly—show your maturity!**
What should you do with clothing after you have looked at it or tried it on? **Fold it like it was or hang it on the hanger again—this respects the store employees!**	If someone in the mall asks you a question, how should you answer? **Look him/her in the eye and answer clearly.**	I want two people to act out respectfully buying something in the store. One of you will be the sales clerk and the other will be the shopper. The rest of us will tell you what you did well and what you can work on.	Should you walk or run in the mall? **Always walk! It may seem like a fun place to run and goof off since it is so big, but the mall is a crowded place. It is important to be civil for the other people there!**
When there is a crowd of people in the mall that you need to get through, you do not shove, but say... **Please excuse me!**	What should you do if you lose the adult you are with when at the mall? **Look for someone from mall security or ask a store clerk to help you.**	When getting on the elevator, do you first wait for people to get off? Act this out for me. **Yes! Stand to the side so they can get off first.**	Show me how you should ride on the elevator or escalator... **Standing still, talking quietly, and keeping hands and feet to yourself!**
If you accidentally spill your drink or food in the food court, you should... **Clean it up! You show your maturity by cleaning up your own messes.**	What should you do after finishing your food in the food court? **Throw your garbage away and make sure your space is clean for the next person to sit there!**	Is it okay to bring food or drink into a store? **No—You should not bring food or drink into a store because it might spill on some of the clothes or products.**	When walking through the mall, it is very important to _____ where you are going! Why? **Watch where you are going! It is easy to bump into other busy shoppers.**

206

Student Activity Sheet - Week 21

Respecting Your Community

Have you ever heard someone speaking disrespectfully to someone working in a store or the mall? How do you think it made them feel?

Name

Student Activity Sheet - Week 22

Respecting Our Country

What do you think it would be like to live in a country where there is very little freedom?

Name

The Star-Spangled Banner

Oh, say can you see
by the dawn's early light
What so proudly we hailed
at the twilight's last gleaming?
Whose broad stripes and bright stars
thru the perilous fight,
O'er the ramparts we watched
were so gallantly streaming?
And the rocket's red glare,
the bombs bursting in air,
Gave proof through the night
that our flag was still there.
Oh, say does that star-spangled
banner yet wave
O'er the land of the free
and the home of the brave?

Student Activity Sheet - Week 23

Reduce, Reuse, Recycle

Fill in the blanks to figure out what this symbol stands for!

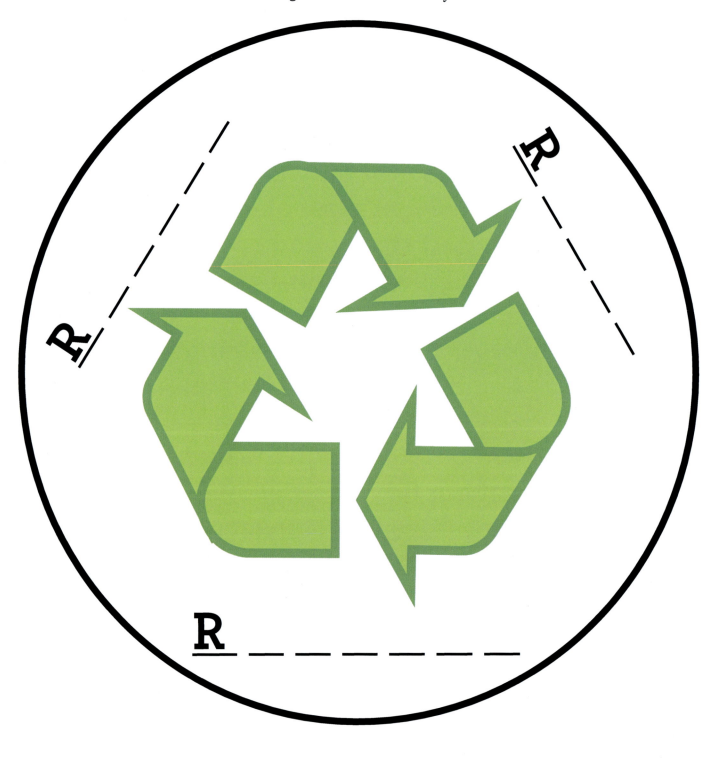

Name

Student Activity Sheet - Week 23

Respecting Our Environment

Have you thought about where the trash goes? Describe what happens to everything you throw away!

Name

Student Activity Sheet - Week 23

What Does This Mean?

Decorate this symbol as you see it on your item from home.
Write the numbers or letters you see.

Describe what you brought to class: _____

What is it made of? _____

Look up the symbol as it appears on your item. What does it mean?

_____

Can you recycle this item? _____

Is this something your family uses often? _____

_____
Name

WEEK 1 **Welcome to Merryville**

Dear Parent/Guardian,

For Your Heart
Common courtesy and respect for others should be part of everyday living. Defining manners as an attitude of the heart that puts the needs of others before your own, Manners of the Heart is here to help you help your child develop respect for others, and in so doing, gain self-respect. You are the one who holds the key to unlock your child's heart. Once the heart is unlocked, your child's mind will open to all that can be learned in the classroom.

Through storytelling, hands-on activities, and role-play, your child will learn the importance of manners and so much more this school year:

- Manners are the foundation for morals.
- Manners are not a set of rules to be followed, but rather principles that guide behavior.
- The attitude behind the action determines the action.

For the Heart of Your Child
At the beginning of each week, your child will bring home a **Home Connection** page. This is your recommended homework, or as we like to call it, "Heartwork". We hope you will make the time to do the suggested activities that reinforce what your child is learning at school. We are confident you'll enjoy the time spent with your child, and even more, your child will enjoy the time spent with you!

This week, we're introducing your child to Merryville, the enchanted town where the Wise Ol' Owl, Wilbur, and his friends live and learn. Through the stories of Merryville, your child will discover that manners come from the heart.

- Ask your child to share this week's Heart Attribute and the definition.
- Encourage your child to say hello to folks you meet.
- Encourage your child to look for the good in others.

Working together, your child can become the lady or gentleman each is meant to be.

From our hearts to yours,

PS Ask your child to share the definition of this week's Heart Attribute, MANNERS, with you.

MANNERS—An attitude of the heart that puts the needs of others ahead of my own

WEEK 2 Introducing Good Deeds

Dear Parent/Guardian,

For Your Heart
In this lesson, we establish the foundation of others-centeredness upon which Manners of the Heart is based. We have found by learning to follow the rules, children develop not only respect for others, but also respect for themselves. Children are learning:

- Rules are opportunities to perform good deeds.
- Why rules are important to learning and growing.
- By helping others learn and grow, they learn and grow too.

Third graders are creating a Class Constitution based on the Manners of the Heart principle of putting the needs of others ahead of your own. They are defining rules for how they will treat each other. Through this exercise, children develop not only respect for others, but also respect for themselves.

For the Heart of Your Child
Why not follow the lead of your child's class and work together to create a Family Constitution using the same three-step process. Gather your children and allow each member of the family to answer the following questions to help form your constitution:

- **ATTITUDES**: What attitudes in our hearts should govern our words and actions?
    - *Treat others the way I want to be treated*
    - *Listen respectfully to what each other has to say*

- **WORDS**: How should we speak to one another?
    - *Always use kind words*
    - *Encourage one another*

- **ACTIONS**: How should we behave ourselves at home?
    - *Follow the rules of the house*
    - *Be generous hosts when company comes*

Write on poster paper or type and print the rules for posting in the kitchen or family area for all to see!

The first and last rule should always be RESPECT!

From our hearts to yours,

PS Ask your child what RESPECT means!

RESPECT—Treating others with dignity

WEEK 3 **Choosing Respect**

Dear Parent/Guardian,

For Your Heart
Respect is at the heart of Manners of the Heart. One of our goals is to help you raise respectful children who become responsible, respectable adults. This week, your child is learning that:

- Showing respect, especially in the face of disrespect, is always the right thing to do.
- Giving respect to everyone, whether they feel respected in return or not.
- Giving respect helps you to gain respect.

For the Heart of Your Child
Using gardening as a model, we believe there are five stages to producing the fruit of respect in your child's life:

1. **Preparing the soil** — Work towards having the same qualities in your own heart that you want to grow in your child's heart. The more you develop mature fruit in your own life, the easier it will be to develop it in your child.

2. **Planting the seeds** — The seeds of honesty, patience, respectfulness, kindness, and gentleness are just a few of the good seeds to cultivate. Gently guide your child to exhibit these qualities by taking each opportunity to teach them. For example, when your child makes a mistake, forgive and teach; when they lie, discuss the need for honesty; when they hurt others, teach about gentleness.

3. **Protecting the growth** — Spend your time making your child feel secure and loved as a member of your family. If your child feels protected, they will have the strength to fight off "pests" and negative influences that can cause disrespect to sprout.

4. **Pruning the branches and pulling the weeds** — Eliminate negative influences as much as possible (such as disrespectful entertainment), and when your child does make mistakes, use repetition to help them remember. For example, if your child forgets to take their plate to the sink after dinner, have him/her practice taking the plate to the sink ten times.

5. **Patiently waiting** — The most difficult stage of gardening involves checking for daily trouble spots and addressing them immediately. By the end of this school year, your child can produce a bounty of respectful fruit when his/her heart is tended by a thoughtful gardener.

From our hearts to yours,

PS Don't forget to ask about this week's Heart Attributes, GOODNESS and RESPECT!

GOODNESS—Being kind, compassionate, and forgiving
RESPECT—Treating others with dignity

WEEK 4 **Helping Others**

Dear Parent/Guardian,

For Your Heart
This week, third graders are developing the ability to put the needs of others ahead of their wants as they learn the following:

- To look for ways to help others.
- To show kindness and love to others by offering to help, such as by being a friend to a lonely child in their class or offering to help with cleanup after a meal at a friend's house.
- Helping others makes the world a better place.

For the Heart of Your Child
Here are a few ways you can support your child's development of helpfulness at home:

1. **Give your child regular duties and hold him or her accountable for taking care of those duties.** When you give your child duties, your child experiences the satisfaction of contributing something valuable to the family.

2. **Assign purposeful duties.** No matter your child's age, any duties you assign should be for one of the following reasons:
   - To help them learn valuable life skills
   - To give your child a valuable role in the family
   - To help your child become a valuable member of society

3. **Assign duties that are age appropriate.** The goal is to help your child find satisfaction in accomplishing a task. Young children have a natural desire to please; you can build on this desire by allowing them to help you. Here are a few age-appropriate duties:
   - Taking out the garbage
   - Setting the table
   - Cleaning the inside of the car
   - Emptying the dishwasher

4. **Take time to show your child how to perform the task.** Children want to perform their tasks well. Lack of successful completion can create frustration.

From our hearts to yours,

PS Don't forget to ask your child to define KINDNESS and LOVE!

LOVE—Genuinely caring for others
KINDNESS—Showing care for others in an unexpected and exceptional way

WEEK 5 **Forgiving Others**

Dear Parent/Guardian,

For Your Heart
This week, third grade students are learning that holding onto unforgiveness does more damage to us and our loved ones than to the person who hurt us. Please consider these Big Ideas:

- A child with a patient and humble heart will be able to both give and receive forgiveness.
- Until they learn patience in excusing the faults of others, children have great difficulty maturing socially or emotionally.
- Humility is cultivated in the heart of a child who learns to ask to be forgiven when at fault.

For the Heart of Your Child
You can teach your child about forgiveness by setting a good example:

1. **Forgive them when they do wrong.** Help your child learn to say, "I'm sorry," after a mistake. Forgive your child quickly when they wrong you, but don't remove the consequences for their misbehavior. Discomfort motivates change. If your child doesn't suffer negative consequences for misbehavior, he won't be inspired to change.

2. **Forgive others when they offend you.** Let your child see you quickly forgive small offenses. Rather than rolling your eyes when cut in line at the grocery or huffing when someone takes the last parking space, be gracious. Wouldn't it be great for your child to hear you say, "They must be in a big hurry," instead of "Who do they think they are?" If you are unforgiving, your child will be unforgiving.

3. **Asking others for forgiveness when you wrong them.** It's never too late to show remorse to someone you've wronged, wounded, offended, or upset. It's important for your child to see you humble yourself and admit when you've been wrong. Be quick to apologize, as well as to forgive.

From our hearts to yours,

PS Don't forget to ask the definitions of PATIENCE and HUMILITY.

HUMILITY—Not caring who gets credit
PATIENCE—Even-tempered endurance

WEEK 6 **Appreciating Others**

Dear Parent/Guardian,

For Your Heart
This week, students are learning to show appreciation for others through kind words and selfless deeds. Third graders are experiencing the joy of sharing their treasure with others, by learning the following:

- How to make others feel appreciated through kind words.
- How to offer words of affirmation to others.
- The more "treasure" one gives away, the more one has to give.

For the Heart of Your Child
As your child is learning how to appreciate others by offering words of encouragement, it is important that your child experiences appreciation at home. Here are small ways to model appreciation for your child:

- Say "thank you" to your children, your spouse, and others in your home.
- Show appreciation for simple pleasures such as good health, nature, good rest, a good meal, etc.
- Try not to complain about minor irritations or wanting things you don't have.
- Try not to miss your child's events, sports, academics, etc.
- Ask your child to find things for which compliments can be given to others—at the grocery store, doctor's office, or in the neighborhood. Make sure your child sees you thank service providers and encourage your child to do the same.
- Send your child a written thank you for an exceptional task completed.

Watching your appreciation of others is the best way for your child to learn to appreciate others, too!

From our hearts to yours,

PS Don't forget to ask the definitions of ENCOURAGEMENT & APPRECIATION.

ENCOURAGEMENT—Offering words to others that builds their confidence
APPRECIATION—Recognizing and acknowledging value in people, places and things

WEEK 7 Being a Buddy, Not a Bully

Dear Parent/Guardian,

For Your Heart
Children have a choice to make – to stand back and allow someone to be bullied, or to step in and stand up by offering help. In this lesson, third graders are learning the following:

- Why it is important to stand up for someone who is being bullied
- What actions to take when they witness bullying
- How to help the bully become a buddy

For The Heart of Your Child
Here are some ways that you can support your child's ability to peacefully resolve bullying situations:

- Talk with your child about a time you witnessed bullying as a child. How did you react? What would you do differently today?

- Explain to your child why it is important to help someone being bullied instead of ignoring it or going along with it. Review the following steps your child is learning at school:
    - Don't stand back.
    - Step in for the one being bullied and ask a friend to join you.
    - Stand up and find a teacher, parent or responsible adult to confront the bully. Sometimes kids who are bullied are scared to ask an adult for help because they think it will make the bullying worse. Kids who know about the bullying can help by going to an adult.

We hope you take the time this week to invest in your child's manners as they learn to step in and stand up for the rights of others.

From our hearts to yours,

PS Don't forget to ask the definitions of KINDNESS & ACCEPTANCE.

KINDNESS—Showing care for others in an unexpected and exceptional way

ACCEPTANCE—Treating everyone you meet with the same respect, regardless of differences

WEEK 8 Following the Golden Rule

Dear Parent/Guardian,

For Your Heart
If your child hasn't already told you, Wise Ol' Wilbur is the central character of Manners of the Heart. The children of Merryville run to Wilbur for guidance and words of wisdom when they can't find their way. He shares his knowledge through sound advice and practical solutions for everyday problems. This week, Wilbur is teaching students about the Golden Rule. Third graders are learning the following:

- The Golden Rule is to treat others the way you want to be treated.
- The Golden Rule is the foundation for helping, forgiving, appreciating, and respecting others.
- The Golden Rule is the beginning of creating a civil society.

For the Heart of Your Child
Children treat others the way they want to be treated when their hearts are filled with love. Love is not just an emotion; it's a choice! As your child learns to practice the Golden Rule with love, you can try one of these fun ways to show love at home this week:

- Fill a book bag or lunchbox for each of your family members with a love note.
- Prepare a special supper of everyone's favorite foods.
- Leave the television off for the evening and enjoy each other's company.
- Give out real hugs and kisses and say "I love you" as you tuck everyone in bed.

Children love others as they have been loved. We hope you find special ways to show love to your children and encourage them to love others by following the Golden Rule!

From our hearts to yours,

PS Ask your child to share the definitions of HUMILITY and EMPATHY.

HUMILITY—Not caring who gets credit
EMPATHY—Walking in another person's shoes

WEEK 9 **Becoming Ladies and Gentlemen**

Dear Parent/Guardian,

For Your Heart
Teaching common courtesies was, at one time, part of a child's upbringing and helped maintain a certain level of order and civility in our society. Without these common courtesies, incivility has become the norm of our culture. We must begin to teach our children basic courtesies because:

- A girl who respects others becomes a lady who respects herself.
- A boy with a kind heart becomes a man with a good heart.
- Habits children develop in childhood help shape who they become as adults and therefore, who we become as a society.

For the Heart of Your Child
This week, your child is learning how to act like a lady or gentleman by caring for the feelings of others. At home, you can remind your child of the following:

- To use respectful language with others at all times
- To show respect for adults
- Girls should allow boys to treat them like ladies
- Boys become gentlemen when they treat a lady like a lady

Watching television together is a great opportunity for discussion about right and wrong behavior. The honoring of others is often represented negatively on television!

Look for moments that allow your child to see you **choose** to be gentle and gracious rather than harsh!

Why is this so important now? Manners instilled in the early years, become morals in the teen years.

From our hearts to yours,

PS Don't forget to ask what GENTLE and GRACIOUS mean.

GENTLE—Speaking and acting with tenderness
GRACIOUS—Being polite, understanding and generous in all situations

WEEK 10 **Being a Host**

Dear Parent/Guardian,

For Your Heart
You don't need a big house with fancy things to be a good host. You only need a heart to serve others and a desire to make others feel better than they did before they came to see you. Learning hospitality teaches generosity – a trait that takes time to develop. Your child is learning that:

- Being a good host shows your guest how much you care.
- Good hosts are generous with their belongings.
- Hospitable hosts make their guests feel loved.

For the Heart of Your Child
This week, create an opportunity for your child to have a friend visit or spend the night. Remember, it does not matter to a child where you live or how messy your house might be. Before the visitor arrives, discuss with your child different ways to be a good host. Make sure your child knows the rules in your home. Here are a few key objectives:

- Allow your child to prepare for the guest.
- Remind your child to allow the guest to choose the activities for the visit.
- Remind your child to walk the guest to the door and thank them for coming.

Providing young children with opportunities to practice being a good host will help instill hospitality and generosity in their hearts for a lifetime, a quality that will serve them well as they learn to see beyond themselves and their circumstances to become all they are meant to be.

From our hearts to yours,

PS Don't forget to ask your child to explain HOSPITALITY and GENEROSITY.

HOSPITALITY—Serving others so they feel comfortable and cared for
GENEROSITY—Gladly giving my time, talent and treasure

WEEK 11 **Being a Guest**

Dear Parent/Guardian,

For Your Heart
In this week's lesson, third graders are learning that guests should behave politely at a party to show gratitude to the host for the invitation. Students are learning:

- To ask politely for something they need
- To participate in activities
- To be kind to everyone at the party

For the Heart of Your Child
Your child is learning that being a good guest is more than being appreciative for an invitation. Being a polite guest is showing how much you care for others.

By helping your child understand that they have responsibilities as a party guest, it helps to ensure that the party will be a success for the host and guests alike. This week, ask your child to share some ways that he or she can be a good guest at the next party. Discuss ways your child can:

- Include others in conversations and activities
- Show appreciation for the host
- Help clean up

We are confident that with a little work and practice, your child can become a pleasant and polite guest.

From Our Hearts to Yours,

PS Don't forget to ask what GRATEFUL and POLITE mean!

GRATEFUL—Giving thanks from the heart
POLITE—Using kind words and actions in all situations

WEEK 12 Greetings and Introductions

Dear Parent/Guardian,

For Your Heart
Children need to learn how to greet others and make introductions because:

- A heart-felt greeting builds a bridge to others; the absence of a friendly greeting builds a wall.
- A smile breaks through almost any language or cultural barrier. When you smile, the world smiles with you.
- Learning how to greet and introduce others helps young children overcome shyness and uneasiness in social settings.

This week, third graders are learning the importance of making a good first impression.

For the Heart of Your Child
Ask your child to teach you the five-step greeting they learned at school, so you can practice it together!

See – Look your new friend in the eye
Smile – Smile as you look at your new friend
Step – Take one step toward the friend as you shake his or her hand
Shake – Grip his or her hand firmly, but not too hard
Speak – Say, "It's nice to meet you."

Other ways you can help reinforce the lesson being learned at school:

- Introduce your child to a new person this week and encourage your child to use the 5 S's! (You may want to explain to the new person that your child is practicing a new skill!)
- Pretend you've never shaken a hand before and allow your child to teach **you** what to do!
- Practice this new skill over and over with your child until it comes naturally.

From Our Hearts to Yours,

PS Ask your child what FRIENDLINESS and MATURITY mean!

FRIENDLINESS—Welcoming others by offering a smile and a kind word
MATURITY—The ability to make the right choice in spite of negative influences

WEEK 13 Encouraging Conversation

Dear Parent/Guardian,

For Your Heart
Everyone has thoughts, ideas, and opinions to share. We show others how much we care for and respect them by the way we participate in conversations. This week, third graders are learning to engage in respectful conversation with others. Students are learning the following:

- To respectfully talk with others by continuing the topic of conversation
- To encourage others through words and body language
- To wait until the other person has completed sharing their thought or opinion

For the Heart of Your Child
You can help reinforce the development of self-control in your child's conversations! Try a few of these quick activities at home this week:

- Help your child understand that conversations involve both people asking and answering questions. Teach your child how to ask questions to start or continue a conversation with another child. Examples might include:
    - When is your birthday?
    - Where did you used to live?
    - What is your favorite food?
    - How many family members do you have?

- Set aside intentional time to listen and talk with your child this week. Take turns asking each other questions and listening to responses. Encourage and praise your child when you notice him or her taking turns contributing to the conversation.

- Have your child practice conversational skills with someone outside of the family this week. Potential conversation partners include a friend, neighbor, doctor or other professional. You may need to help your child start the conversation. Remind your child to ask questions and encourage the other person with polite words and body language.

Throughout the week, pay close attention to times when your child listens well and asks questions with others. Be sure to thank your child for listening during conversations.

From Our Hearts to Yours,

PS Don't forget to ask your child about SELF-CONTROL and PARTICIPATION!

SELF-CONTROL—The ability to manage yourself when no one is looking

PARTICIPATION—Choosing to be fully involved in the task or project at hand

WEEK 14 **Using the Phone**

Dear Parent/Guardian,

For Your Heart
This week, we are working on telephone manners.

- Phone manners are much more than learning how to make and take calls.
- Children gain responsibility in other areas of life when they learn to use the phone responsibly.
- Learning how and when to use the phone protects children from the risk of overuse and addiction.

Third graders are developing consideration for others by learning how to use the phone respectfully.

For the Heart of Your Child
Here are some ways to reinforce your child's new learning this week:

- Ask your child to describe *Getting to Know You*, a Merryville story about two friends, Sarah and Allie. Sarah and Allie learn that their relationship is based mainly on the texting and calling they do on their phones. They discover they need to spend time really getting to know one another.
- This week, your child is thinking about **No Phone Zones**, places where it is better to not be on a phone. Ask your third grader to name some of these zones! Here are some of the ones we talked about:
    - Library
    - Restaurant
    - Movies
    - Family Dinner Table
    - Car
- Spending less time in front of a screen and more time getting to know those we love is good for all of us!

From Our Hearts to Yours,

PS Don't forget to ask what RESPONSIBILITY and COURTESY mean!

RESPONSIBILITY—Following through on your duties without supervision
COURTESY—Respectful and well-mannered words and actions toward others

WEEK 15 **Writing From the Heart**

Dear Parent/Guardian,

For Your Heart
This week, your child is developing the valuable skill of written communication. Third graders are learning to express their thoughtfulness in a hand-written note. Children are learning to recognize appropriate times to communicate through writing, such as to encourage others or express their feelings:

- To recognize appropriate times to communicate through writing
- To encourage others through writing
- To show thoughtfulness for others by giving them a card

For the Heart of Your Child
You can reinforce your child's development of this thoughtfulness at home. Try these activities this week:

- Your child is writing a letter in class this week. Ask who the letter has been written for and help them deliver it.
- Teach your child how to express thankfulness for birthday or Christmas gifts by writing a card to each person from whom they receive a gift. Help your child address and mail the card.
- Spend time writing a letter to your child this week, as a means of modeling appropriate written communication. In the letter, share with your child the joys that he or she brings to your life.

We know that with your help at home, your child will become an expressive communicator through thoughtful writing.

From Our Hearts to Yours,

PS Don't forget to ask what THOUGHTFUL and EXPRESSIVE mean to your child.

THOUGHTFUL—Looking for ways to make others feel loved
EXPRESSIVE—Revealing the content of your heart

WEEK 16 **Respecting Adults**

Dear Parent/Guardian,

For Your Heart
This week, children are learning there are many adults in the community who are concerned about their safety and must be respected. Third graders are learning to respect adult leaders by following *Wilbur's Words of Wisdom*:

- **A** Answer questions.
- **D** Do what they say.
- **U** Use their correct title.
- **L** Listen and look them in the eye.
- **T** Turn your frown right side up.
- **S** Say "Sir" and "Ma'am."

For the Heart of Your Child
Here are a few ways to reinforce what your child is learning about respecting adults:

- Discuss the importance of showing respect and appreciation for adults in your community.
- Remind your child to use polite words whenever speaking to adults.
- Thank your child when you see him being respectful to an adult.
- Lead by example by respecting authority figures in your community.

Insist on respectful speech and attitudes when your child interacts with adults. You'll raise a child that everyone loves!

From Our Hearts to Yours,

PS Don't forget to ask your child to explain HONOR and OBEDIENCE!

HONOR—Valuing the worth of another by showing respect
OBEDIENCE—Choosing to submit to authority

WEEK 17 **Respecting the Team**

Dear Parent/Guardian,

For Your Heart
In this week's lessons, students are learning that being a valuable team player involves putting the good of the team ahead of themselves. In this lesson, third graders are learning the following:

- A good sport wins well and loses well.
- A good sport does not make other people feel bad when they lose.
- A good sport does not get upset when he or she loses.
- Being a good sport makes the game more fun for everyone.

For the Heart of Your Child
You can help your child develop sportsmanship and cooperation. Here are some activities to reinforce what your child is learning at school:

- Discuss what happens when someone is not being a good teammate, compared to what happens when everyone works together.
- While watching a sporting event with your child, call attention to team members who are being good team players.
- Help your child learn not to take winning or losing too seriously by being a good sport yourself!

From Our Hearts to Yours,

PS Don't forget to ask your child to explain COOPERATION and SPORTSMANSHIP!

SPORTSMANSHIP— Being more concerned with supporting your team than helping yourself

COOPERATION—Working with others for everyone's best; choosing to be helpful, not hurtful

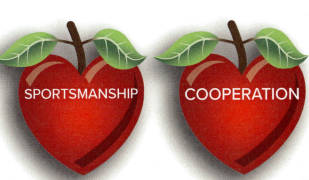

WEEK 18 **Respecting Differences**

Dear Parent/Guardian,

For Your Heart
Young children who develop the ability to look at others with the eyes of their hearts won't allow differences to become obstacles in getting to know and love those who are different. This week, third graders are learning the following:

- We come from many different cultures and backgrounds.
- People from other cultures view our ways as different from their own, just as we view theirs as different from ours.
- We should always show respect for different cultures and ethnicities.

For the Heart of Your Child
Here are some ideas to support your child's appreciation for cultural differences:

- Share the history and background of your family. Are there any interesting customs that your family enjoys? Help your child write a short paragraph about your family's heritage to share with their class.
- On your next trip to the grocery store, take a few minutes to look at the wide variety of foods from many cultures and talk with your child about the different ethnicities in your community.
- Ask your child how he would want people to respond to him, if he were in a different country and looked different than the local folks.
- Discuss respectful behavior when you see someone dressed differently than you.

The more you talk with your child about having respect for others who are different, the more their heart (and yours) will grow!

From Our Hearts to Yours,

PS Don't forget to ask your child to explain UNDERSTANDING and ACCEPTANCE.

UNDERSTANDING—Looking at others and listening to others without judgment

ACCEPTANCE—Treating everyone you meet with the same respect, regardless of differences

WEEK 19 **Respecting Privacy**

Dear Parent/Guardian,

For Your Heart
Learning how gossip hurts everyone—the one who is talked about and the one doing the talking—teaches children to choose their words carefully. This week, third graders are learning the following:

- What gossiping really is and why it is hurtful to others.
- What to do if friends are gossiping.
- Why it is important to keep a friend's secret.
- When someone is in danger, it's not gossiping to share with an adult.
- When it is okay to tell an adult about an incident.

For the Heart of Your Child
Take time at home this week to reinforce what your child is learning about gossiping at school:

- Share a personal experience with your child about a time someone spread gossip about you. Talk about how it made you feel. Invite your child to share a similar experience with you.
- Talk with your child about the difference between keeping someone's confidence or secret and reporting when someone is in danger. Remind your child that he/she needs to care for friends by sharing dangerous secrets with a trusted adult.
- Share an embarrassing moment with your child. Tell your child you are trusting him/her to keep your moment a secret and that you know he/she is trustworthy enough to do it. You will empower your child by sharing a secret and saying you trust him/her.
- Set a good example for your child by respecting others' privacy yourself, not eavesdropping and refraining from gossip.

From Our Hearts to Yours,

PS Don't forget to ask your child to define CONSIDERATE and TRUSTWORTHY!

CONSIDERATE—Taking into account the feelings of others before you speak or act
TRUSTWORTHY—Doing what you said you would do when you said you would do it

WEEK 20 **Respecting Property**

Dear Parent/Guardian,

For Your Heart
This week, children are learning about respecting the property of others. The focus for third grade is understanding the importance of doing their own work rather than copying someone else's work—respect for the intellectual property of others. Third graders are learning:

- The full understanding of cheating and why it is important not to cheat.
- How it feels to have someone else take credit for their work.
- How to help someone else with their work without cheating.

For the Heart of Your Child
Here are suggestions for you to reinforce what your child is learning about respecting others' work:

- Help your child with homework without giving the answers. Explain that when parents give the answers, that is cheating too and doesn't help anyone. Share with your child how it can be harder to help someone the right way, which gives a greater reward in the end.
- Talk to your child about what to do and say when a friend asks him or her to cheat. Standing up to friends is very difficult for children at this age. Remind your child to use the school rules and your family rules against cheating as their reason for not cheating – until he or she is ready to say "no" for his own reasons.
- If your child's class created a policy on cheating, ask your child to explain the class rules to you. Discuss why the policy is important and how proud you will be of your child's commitment to follow the policy.
- The next time you hear a news story about an athlete, politician, or professional who cheated, talk with your child about some of the more serious consequences of cheating (being penalized from the team, jail time, etc.).

From Our Hearts to Yours,

PS Don't forget to ask about APPRECIATION and RESPONSIBILITY!

APPRECIATION—Recognizing and acknowledging value in people, places and things
RESPONSIBILITY—Following through on your duties without supervision

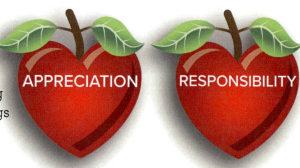

WEEK 21 **Respecting Our Community**

Dear Parent/Guardian,

For Your Heart
This week, children are learning what it means to respect their community by understanding they are a part of something bigger than themselves. Children are learning that "we're all in this together"—in the classroom, school and community.

- Civility shows respect for others in your community.
- Communities function more smoothly, efficiently, and pleasantly when both adults and children practice common respect for others.
- Respectful communities count on the reinforcement of respectful behavior in classrooms.

This week, third graders are learning about civility by learning to act respectfully at the mall.

For the Heart of Your Child
To reinforce what your child is learning at school this week, make a "Just Act Respectfully" jar by cutting out the scenarios below and placing them in a large jar. At the dinner or breakfast table, pull a couple of slips out of the jar and lead a family discussion on the best way to deal with the situation. You can also add things you're doing with for discussions on civility.

From Our Hearts to Yours,

MANNERS of the HEART

PS Don't forget to ask what CIVIL and APPROPRIATE mean!

| Should you walk or run in the mall? Walk | When there is a crowd of people in the mall that you need to get through, you do not shove, but rather say… Excuse me! | What should you do if you lose the adult you are with at the mall? Find an adult who works in the store or mall by looking for a name badge and ask for help. | When getting on the elevator, do you first wait for people to get off? You allow people to get off before entering the elevator. |

CIVIL—To respect others and self for the betterment of community
APPROPRIATE—Knowing the right thing to say or do in any given situation

WEEK 22 **Respecting Our Country**

Dear Parent/Guardian,

For Your Heart
Being an American citizen is a great honor. With that honor comes great responsibility. Instilling patriotism in children through the appreciation for our soldiers creates a desire to become a good citizen. This week, third graders are learning the following:

- Americans throughout history have fought for our freedom
- Ways we can show appreciation for members of our armed services
- How to be good citizens who respect our country and all that she stands for

When we teach children to appreciate those who defend our country, we help them develop appreciation for the freedoms of our country.

For the Heart of Your Child
You can help instill respect for the freedoms we enjoy in our country in the heart of your child. Here are some ideas to reinforce your child's development of respect for our military and our country:

- Whenever you encounter someone in military uniform, look them in the eye, nod and say "Thank you for your service" with your whole heart and teach your children to do the same.
- It's easy to criticize our president or other leaders, or to complain about all that is wrong with our country. Do your best to show appreciation and respect for the country that gives opportunities to succeed like no other.
- Participate in Veteran's Day events with your children. Most are free and open to the public.

Despite our flaws and struggles, we ought to show gratitude and respect for the country we call home.

's,

PS Don't forget to ask what PATRIOTISM and CITIZENSHIP mean!

PATRIOTISM—Loving our country enough to protect it and the principles upon which it was founded

CITIZENSHIP—An attitude of cooperation and social responsibility

WEEK 23 Respecting Our Environment

Dear Parent/Guardian,

For Your Heart
This week, children are learning to respect the environment for the sake of all of us. Third graders are recognizing they have a part to play in keeping their environment clean, so everyone can enjoy the beauty of their surroundings, indoors and outdoors. They are learning:

- Why it is important to take care of our surroundings to show appreciation to others who worked so hard to create it and maintain it
- What we can do to add beauty to our environment
- Taking care of the environment around you makes your heart feel good

For the Heart of Your Child
Here are a few ideas for how you can reinforce what your child is learning:

- Keep your room at home neat and clean.
- Help take care of your home by cleaning and sweeping.
- Never leave a mess you make (no matter where you are!)
- Thank the custodian for working hard to keep the school clean.
- Take care of our city by not littering.
- Walk on sidewalks, never walk across flowerbeds.
- Leave the flowers for others to enjoy rather than picking them for yourself.
- Pick up litter even if you're not the one who dropped it.
- Tell an adult if you see someone hurting property.

Teach your child that all of us are responsible for the care of our environment. When everyone respects his or her surroundings, there can be beauty everywhere!

From Our Hearts to Yours,

PS Don't forget to ask what CONSCIENTIOUS and RESOURCEFUL mean.

CONSCIENTIOUS—Diligently careful
RESOURCEFUL—Finding creative solutions to everyday problems; using your imagination and mind to repurpose materials

Made in the USA
Columbia, SC
21 August 2021